From the Model T to Mars

From the Model T to Mars

Dr. Bill Sherman

1845BOOKS

Cover design by *the*BookDesigners
Cover photographs courtesy of the Sherman family
Book design by Kasey McBeath

The Library of Congress has cataloged this book under paperback ISBN 978-1-4813-1964-5.

Library of Congress Control Number: 2023902584

I must say words of deepest appreciation to Debbie, our daughter, and Tim, her husband. They have been incredibly supportive of Veta and me through the years. They have also been generous supporters of Truett Seminary. David, our youngest son, has been such a help as well. Both children live nearby and have made a difference in our well-being in our senior years. Their care has been keenly appreciated. Let us face it—family is special.

CONTENTS

FOREWORD

Dwight L. Moody is frequently credited for saying, "The world has yet to see what God will do with a man fully consecrated to him." That may well be true. That being said, in *From the Model T to Mars* you will read of Bill Sherman's life and ministry and will marvel and revel in what the Lord has done with his yielded and devoted life.

A chief joy of my job as dean of Baylor University's George W. Truett Theological Seminary is to spend copious amounts of time with ministers of various ages and at various stages in their gospel work and witness. In recent years, I have been blessed beyond measure to get to know well Bill and Veta Sherman and their daughter, Deborah. In no small measure, this ministerial memoir emerged from extensive conversations that we had together over time in Nashville, Tennessee and Waco, Texas.

Speaking of time, perhaps the most striking aspect of Bill Sherman's ministry is its *longevity*, some sixty-six years all told! Far more than marking or biding time, however, what readers will discover in this valuable volume (in addition to a remarkable memory and memorable stories) are the character qualities that enabled such a protracted ministry: *fidelity, integrity, industry, magnanimity*, and not a little *levity*.

Please do me a favor. Set aside the time necessary to read the ministry autobiography of Bill Sherman. It will be time well spent and will bring both pleasure and profit. Ever self-effacing, not even Bill would seek to deny the impact that the Lord has had through his eventful life and fruitful ministry. What one discovers in *From the Model T to Mars* is a role model for ministry in the words of one who was unflinchingly and indefatigably committed to ministry for life.

Todd D. Still
Waco, Texas on the 3rd day of Christmas 2022

PREFACE

For several years various friends and family members have said to me, "Bill, you ought to write your life story." I appreciated their interest; however, I did not see that my life as a pastor was any different from hundreds of other Baptist preachers. I responded, "Who would read it?" Then one of my friends mentioned something that I had not considered. He said, "Bill, you had a ministry of sixty-six years. Most pastors have a ministry of forty to forty-five years. Your ministry has been twenty years longer than the average pastor. You have served in six churches in three different states. Your churches have been outstanding in volunteer mission involvements and in support of the Lottie Moon and Home Mission Offerings. Your church in Nashville led the way in bridge-building in race relations. Ned McWherter, Governor of Tennessee, said that you were the 'conscience of Middle Tennessee' on moral issues. I believe that young pastors would benefit from reading your story." His statement allowed me to see things from a different vantage point, and I reconsidered. When my daughter and her husband gave words of encouragement as well, I decided to write my story.

Rolling back the years and reliving experiences over the past nine decades of my life has been gratifying. I have appreciated my experiences more the second time around and have been more grateful to my family and extended family than I was back then. The value of being raised in a Christian home cannot be overstated. The spiritual tutoring of Polytechnic Baptist Church in Fort Worth, Texas, was foundational to my life. The pastor, Dr.

Baker James Cauthen, baptized me in 1938. My greater family—
grandparents, uncles, aunts, and cousins—all lived in the Fort
Worth area and were active church members; churchmanship has
always been important to my family. Being raised in a Christian
home gave me four strikes at the plate of life instead of three.

My brother, Cecil, and my sister, Ruth, went to Baylor University before me. My five years at Baylor not only shaped me
but strengthened my faith, as well. I met my wonderful wife of
sixty-nine years, Veta, at Baylor. She has helped to strengthen my
faith, as well, and has been a blessing to the churches that we have
served. Our three children—Donny, Debbie, and David—have
been wonderful blessings. The Psalms rightly say, "Children are a
blessing and a gift from the Lord" (Ps 127:3 CEV).

The professors at Southwestern Baptist Theological Seminary helped to shape the direction of my ministry. Dr. T.B. Maston was an inspiration to me and helped form my commitment
to challenge the ills of the social order. This was particularly true
regarding race relations.

The country church in Malone, Texas, that I served for four
years, patiently suffered through the novice sermons I preached.
We loved each other—all forty-one members of us. For two years
I served as Minister of Music, Education, and Youth at First
Baptist, Bonham, Texas. The church members were good to us
and allowed me to finish my basic seminary degree. After Bonham I served in the same position for four years at First Baptist,
McKinney, Texas. The membership was wonderful. I finished my
advanced seminary degrees in those years.

In 1963, our lives and ministry then took a significant turn.
Veta and I had initially felt that missions was our calling. However,
a phone call from University Heights Baptist Church changed our
focus. The church was one block from Oklahoma State University
in Stillwater, Oklahoma. They needed a pastor. We were surprised
and wondered if this was a door God had opened. After prayer-
ful analysis, we felt that it was. We moved to Stillwater in May
1963 and had four and a half years of exciting ministry there. In
those years we had the joy of seeing lives changed and students

challenged in discipleship. We took groups to Glorieta Baptist Assembly each year, and two of our students became Journeymen through the Foreign Mission Board.

Then in 1967, another phone call changed our lives when the chairman of the pulpit committee at Woodmont Baptist Church, in Nashville, Tennessee, called. After careful deliberations, we felt that the Lord was leading us to Woodmont. We moved in December 1967. The next thirty years were incredibly fulfilling.

The church developed a television ministry. We also began a joint service that would last for twenty-seven years with one of the largest African American Baptist churches in Nashville—the Fifteenth Avenue Baptist Church. Our church members fulfilled over nine hundred short-term mission assignments around the world. Our Lottie Moon offerings exceeded $100,000 for over a dozen years. Our Sunday School grew from 400 to 1,500. Each of these blessings was thanks to the goodness of the Lord. Veta and I had a great ride at Woodmont for thirty years and were blessed beyond measure.

Our lives were not always upbeat. We lost our oldest son, Donny, to cancer in 2015. I experienced metastatic melanoma from 1995 to 2005. By the grace of God and Dr. Sewa Legha at MD Anderson, in Houston, Texas, I remain cancer-free as of this writing. I retired from Woodmont on January 1, 1998.

In 2001, our ministry took another turn. The First Baptist Church of Fairview, Tennessee, called and asked if I would preach for them the following Sunday. I did. They asked me to become their pastor. We were together for the next nineteen and a half years. The church was able to make improvements in the facilities that ranged from constructing a new education building to renovating the church house twice to adding lighted paved parking lots. The members were grand folk. We retired when the COVID outbreak became widespread in 2020. I was eighty-eight and blessed to be in good health. We left the church debt-free and with a generous balance of funds in the bank.

This has been an overview of my sixty-six years in the ministry. Was it all peaches and cream? No. There were times that were a sticky wicket. We dealt with them. We had times of testing. But God saw us through the minefields.

I would like to express gratitude to those who have helped me along the way. Dr. Ralph Lynn, my Baylor history professor, inspired me. Dr. T.B. Maston provided me with great direction at Southwestern. Frances Lawrence was a wonderful help in McKinney. Roger and Pat Tucker were an inspiration through the years at Stillwater. Joanne James was my secretary at Woodmont for twenty-seven years and a good one. Dean and Lois Shelton were and are true anchors of the church in Fairview. My wife, Veta, has been an inspiration to me, not only as a wife, but also as an advisor in each church setting. She meant as much to every church in which I served as I did. Our three children have been a remarkable blessing through the years. Our six grandchildren and our two great-grandchildren are special. I also want to thank Woodmont Baptist Church for allowing me to research in their Heritage Room. Dr. Alan Lefever and his wife Sara have been extremely helpful through it all. Dean Todd Still of Truett Seminary has been a friend and encourager of this project.

As I look back in retrospect, Veta and I agree that we would be happy to serve at any of our former churches again. It has been a long way to Tipperary, but we are happy to have taken the journey. In closing, I hope that this book will give young pastors help and encouragement in their ministries. For the pulpit owes the pew one thing—to preach the truth courageously.

Dr. Bill Sherman

1
THE EARLY YEARS

The 1930s

I discovered America on March 3, 1932, in Fort Worth, Texas. My parents were John and Annie Mae Sherman. Daddy was thirty-one when I arrived; my mother was twenty-seven; my brother, Cecil, was four; and my sister, Ruth, was two. Our address, where I lived for the next eighteen years, was 2818 Avenue F. The neighborhood was blue-collar, and most of the houses had been built in the late nineteenth century.

Polytechnic, frequently shortened to Poly, had initially been a small town on the outskirts of Fort Worth. Eventually the city grew and absorbed the community. However, Poly retained a small-town atmosphere with its own stores, post office, theatre, schools, and churches. One could easily stay there for weeks without going to Fort Worth, though a streetcar did connect Poly to downtown.

Daddy's oldest sister, Hester, who married I.W. Parker, lived next door to us. We called them Uncle Bill and Aunty-Grandma, a title given to her by Cecil. Daddy's mother died in 1926, which left us with only one grandmother. Cecil asked Hester if she would be both our aunt and grandmother. She graciously consented, and the title stuck. They, along with their daughters, Eunice and Lois, lived next door to us for the next ten years and were a wonderful Christian influence on us.

The world I entered in 1932 was in turmoil. In the presidential election, Franklin D. Roosevelt had just defeated President Herbert Hoover. The United States was in the midst of the Great Depression, and twelve million citizens were out of work. The

Dow Jones hit a low of forty-one. Fascism was looming on the horizon in Germany and Italy. Japan had invaded Manchuria and was headed to China. I knew nothing of the above. However, considering the economy, I have often wondered if my mother and daddy were all that glad to see me. Another mouth to feed? Another child to clothe?[1] Granted, that question was never posed. Every signal they ever sent me was one of acceptance, love, and encouragement! I am so thankful for my parents, and I cherish their memories.

My home church was Poly Baptist where Baker James Cauthen was pastor for the first seven years of my life. He was also a missions professor at Southwestern Baptist Theological Seminary. Brother Cauthen was an outstanding preacher and quite personable. Mother was the Sunday School superintendent of the junior department (ages nine to twelve); and Daddy led the singing in opening assembly, filled out the records, and served as a substitute teacher. Church was as regular for our family as the sun coming up in the east and going down in the west. The three building blocks of my life were home, church, and school; these three institutions shaped the person I came to be.

One of my earliest memories occurred when I was four. We lived in a wooden frame house built in the 1880s with five rooms and a bathroom. There was wallpaper in each room and linoleum on the floors of the kitchen and dayroom. When a winter cold front (what we called a "norther") came through, blasting cold air, the wallpaper would breathe and the linoleum would rise and fall. Since the five rooms did not offer enough bedroom space, Daddy employed a carpenter, Mr. Brown, to add a long bedroom across the back of the house. He and a helper did all the work with hand tools, which fascinated me. I noticed that every time Mr. Brown needed something he said, "Bring me the damn saw," or "Hand me the damn board." This went on all day long. I had never heard that word before and figured "damn" must be an important word. Suppertime came, and we gathered around a

---

[1]   In 1932 when I was born, a loaf of bread was seven cents, and a gallon of gas was nine cents. A car cost $610 and a new house cost $6,510. The average American income was $1,650 a year.

This is my father and my older brother and sister in 1936. The picture was taken at the Botanical Gardens in Fort Worth. I am four years old.

small enamel-covered table. After Daddy said the blessing, I sat straight up and said, "Pass me the damn peas." I was so proud of myself until I looked at Daddy. He squinted his eyes and gave me a look that almost stopped my heart. Mother sprang out of her chair, reached across the table, grabbed me by the ear, and dragged me to the bathroom. All along the way I screamed and cried, "Why? Why?" She washed my mouth out with soap and said, "Billy Boy, we do not use that kind of language in our family." A few days passed before I resumed my post and watched Mr. Brown at work again.

Another event that took place when I was four was the widening and paving of the road in front of our house. One morning we were awakened by the noise of construction machines. Steam shovels, steam rollers, and dump trucks were everywhere. Avenue F was becoming East Rosedale—a main artery that would go west from Poly to the south side of Fort Worth. Our gravel street would now be four lanes paved with red bricks. For over six months I sat in our front porch swing and watched the progress. The workers were friendly and gave me chewing gum from time to time; I took cold water to them. They added a curb and put in a concrete side-walk as well. To top it off, President Roosevelt came riding down the finished street in 1937. Our entire family stood on the front porch as a dozen policemen on motorcycles rode by with sirens blaring. The President was behind them in an open convertible, waving his straw hat from side to side. We watched until they were out of sight. Then Daddy said, "Kids, that was the President of the United States. Don't ever forget this day!" And we did not.

Another experience that I have never forgotten occurred when I was six. Cecil and I came home from the movies on Saturday afternoon, and a metal rowboat with a small outboard motor was lying in our driveway. We went inside and asked Daddy about it. He said, "Boys, I bought this boat and motor at Montgomery Ward so we can go out to Lake Worth and fish together." We already had an old trailer, and the 1929 Chevy Coupe had a trailer hitch, so we were ready to go. Every Saturday that our calendar was clear and the weather was good, Daddy, Cecil, and I drove out to Lake Worth nine miles west of town. After unloading the boat into the water, we parked the car and trailer at a nearby picnic pavilion. We fished all day, swam in the lake, returned to the pavilion, loaded the boat, and headed for home.

One afternoon we returned to the pavilion to find somebody had let the air out of all the tires in the car and trailer. Daddy reached into the trunk and pulled out a small hand pump to inflate the tires. He pumped and pumped. The sun was hot as blazes. After finishing just one tire, he was wringing wet. Cecil said, "Daddy, let me do one." He picked up the handle, put his entire weight on the pump, and was left dangling in the air. Daddy took over again. After pumping up one more tire, Daddy stood straight and blew up. "If I could get my hands on those sons of bitches . . ." Then he paused. Cecil and I were in shock. I had never seen Daddy like this, and I had never heard those words before. I had no idea what they meant. We were very quiet. Finally, after about an hour Daddy had enough air in the six tires to ease up to a Texaco station off the Jacksboro Highway, inflate the tires, and head home. We drove in the driveway about 8:00 p.m., and Daddy sent me inside to tell

Mother and Ruth that we were all right. I ran into the house, and Mother exclaimed, "Where have you been? I was about to call the police." Innocently, I responded, "Daddy said some sons of bitches let all the air out of the tires on the car and trailer. That's why we are late." Mother turned white. Ruth said, "You dummy!" Mother slapped me so hard I saw stars, and I burst into tears. She said, "Go tell John I need to talk to him!" I went running out of the house and across the yard crying. When I got to the garage, Cecil and Daddy were lifting the boat to hang on the rafters above the car. Daddy stopped and asked, "Why are you crying?" I replied, "Because Mother slapped me." He asked, "Why?" I answered, "I don't know. All I did was tell her that you said some sons of bitches let all the air out of the tires." Daddy stopped and sighed. Taking a deep breath, he looked up into the sky and said, "That's all I needed." We ate a late supper that night in silence. Innocence is refreshing. It is a shame we lose it.

In 1937 I started kindergarten in the basement of Poly Elementary. Ruth was on the first floor in the second grade, and

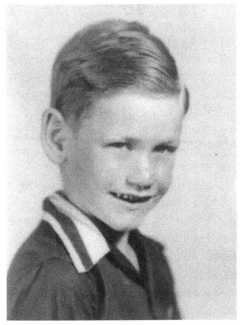

A picture of me, age four, in a favorite navy shirt.

We three kids in 1937
in the backyard.

Cecil was on the second floor in the fourth grade. Mother and Daddy had attended high school in this very building which now housed the elementary students. Poly Baptist Church was right behind our school. William James Junior High School was one block to the north, and the new Poly High School was a block and a half to the west of our house. We kids walked to church and school all the years we were growing up.

In 1938 I was in the first grade with Mrs. Williams as my teacher. The most significant event in my life that year was that I became a Christian. I had been to every Sunday morning and evening worship service, to all Wednesday night prayer meetings, and to each revival held in our church. If an event was happening at Poly Baptist, our family attended. I watched as my older brother and sister invited Jesus into their hearts and were baptized. I told Mother and Daddy my feelings, and on a Saturday morning Daddy took a Bible, and we sat down on the bed in the room that Mr. Brown had built. Daddy turned to John 3:16, which I knew by heart, and asked if I was ready to give my heart to Jesus. I said a tearful "Yes," and then I prayed, and Daddy prayed. The moment was a tender one. The following Sunday morning during the invitational hymn, I went forward to Brother Cauthen. At the next baptismal service, he baptized me. I remember the moment like it was yesterday.

In 1939 Brother Cauthen shared with the church that he felt the Lord calling him to serve as a missionary in China. For all these years he had been speaking to seminary students about being sensitive to God's call, and now God had spoken to him. His wife, Eloise, was the daughter of the Glasses, who were currently serving as missionaries in China. Although the church deeply loved our pastor, everyone encouraged him to follow the Lord's leadership.

A few days later Daddy, Cecil, and I were waiting to get a haircut at the Poly barbershop. The barber who was cutting Brother Cauthen's hair said to our pastor, "Baker, I hear you are leaving the church and going to China as a missionary. Is this true?" Brother Cauthen answered, "Yes, it's true." The barber said, "Baker, I want you to think about this. The church is growing, and you are a good preacher and a popular professor at the seminary. If you stay home and play your cards right, you could either be the pastor of the largest church in town or president of the seminary. Why do you want to go to China and throw your life away?" His question stunned me as a seven-year-old. Brother Cauthen gently replied, "I am going to China because that is what I feel the Lord wants me to do with my life." That was the end of the conversation. On the way home Daddy talked to Cecil and me about what we had heard. "Boys, you need to listen to Christ and no one else as you live your lives." That really made an impression on me. The Cauthens left our church in 1939.

Outside of church activities, what was our daily life like in the 1930s? From 1928 to 1945 we always had a cow enclosed in a red picket fence in our backyard. Each morning Daddy milked the cow. When Cecil was born in 1927, my grandfather told Mother and Daddy that Cecil was going to need plenty of milk to grow strong bones; so, he gave us a Jersey cow named Goatie. I can barely

Sunday evening worship at Polytechnic Baptist Church, Dr. Baker James Cauthen, Pastor, 1938.

remember her; but one of her calves was Beauty, whom I remember quite well. After he finished the milking, Daddy would fill three bowls full of milk for all the dogs and cats in the neighborhood.

On Friday nights we either took in a Poly ballgame or went to the New Liberty Theatre to see Gene Autry and Smiley Burnette in a cowboy movie. Mother loved to hear Gene Autry sing. On other weeknights we listened to the radio, for in those days radio was king. Our favorite programs were *The Aldrich Family*, *Fibber McGee and Molly*, *Dr. I.Q.*, and *The Lone Ranger*. Mother never let us listen to *Gang Busters* as she feared that show was a bad influence on us. Other nights Daddy entertained us with songs and stories. He loved to sing "Walk Tom Wilson Walk," "The Cat Came Back," and "Casey Jones." I heard those songs so many times that I can still sing every word. We also had an old player piano that required clipping in the song roll and pumping two foot pedals to play the tune. Our favorite songs were "Twelfth Street Rag," "Three O'clock in the Morning," and "A Perfect Day." On rainy days in the summer Cecil, Ruth, and I played Monopoly all day.

My first memory of a movie was *Flash Gordon* on a Saturday morning at the Varsity. The Varsity Theatre was two blocks from our house in the Poly business district. The shows were nine cents before 6:00 p.m. and eleven cents afterward. Littering was commonplace back then, and people discarded their cold drink bottles everywhere. Stores paid a penny for each returned bottle. Collecting bottles was a piece of cake for me; I could find nine bottles anytime I wanted to, which allowed me to get into the show for free. The movie that really impressed me was *Gone with The Wind*. To a seven-year-old it was almost overwhelming. However, my favorite movie of this period was *Snow White and the Seven Dwarfs*. I walked home singing, "'Hi ho, hi ho, it's off to work we go . . .'" The shows were a diversion—an escape from the tough times everyone was experiencing in those years. Movie houses were also air-conditioned and provided relief from the stifling summer heat for two hours at a time. In addition, movies were affordable to just about everyone.

On Sunday afternoons we faithfully drove to the farm and visited with my mother's parents, Dad Brannon and Bamaw. Mother's sister and brother also lived in Fort Worth and frequently joined us with their families. Mother's sister, Ruth, married Claude Williamson and had three children—Marshall, Shirleen, and Betty K. Mother's younger brother, John, married Ann Marvel and had two children—John Jr. and Patricia Ann. When we all got together, we played softball or pitched horseshoes or washers. The boys had corncob fights—one team in the barn, the other outside. In August or September, we pulled watermelon and had a watermelon cutting.

In the summertime Daddy rented a cabin at Lake Worth for two weeks where we swam and fished to our hearts' content. We also set a trotline and caught catfish. We saved the fish and invited all the family for a big fish fry on the last Saturday of our trip. We looked forward to this vacation every summer.

In Fort Worth one hundred degrees plus was not uncommon. Residential air-conditioning in our neighborhood was a pipe dream. After supper most of our neighbors came out onto their front porches, sat in rocking chairs or swings, and visited with each other while the houses cooled down. All the windows in the houses were left open. The kids played red rover, hide and seek, or capture the flag. About 8:30 or 9:00 p.m., folks went in to hear the news on the radio and then turn in. The buzzing of a mosquito around your ear was not an unusual sound to hear in the dark. Daddy would come in with the FLIT spray, which usually got the mosquito but half-nigh choked us.

Winters were cold, and our bedroom had no heat. My older brother, Cecil, and I slept in the same bed from the time I discovered America until he went to Baylor in 1945. Mind you, this was not a king-sized bed. The back room of our house had three beds lined up against the inner wall. Mother and Daddy slept in the first one. My sister, Ruth, slept in the second one, which was a three-quarter sized bed. Cecil and I slept in the third one in the corner of the room. We three kids all wore flannel pajamas. Before bedtime we would stand in front of a gas stove with grates in it, turn round and round to get the flannel warm, and then make a dash for the covers in the frigid bedroom. Cecil was four years older than I was. He would jump into the middle of the bed and then roll to the wall, taking virtually all the covers with him. I would naturally complain and ask him to move over! My requests fell on deaf ears. About this time each night, Daddy would say, "You boys get quiet, or I'm coming over there." So, I just hushed and shivered. One night I decided to get revenge. I clipped a safety pin to my pajamas. Cecil and I both made the run for it with the same old results. I quietly reached for the safety pin, straightened it into a dagger, gently lifted the cover, and . . . Touché! Cecil bounced off the wall hollering, "Ouch!" I delighted in my mischief. He then elbowed me, took virtually all the covers, and yelled, "STOP IT!" Daddy demanded that we stop, or he was coming over there. We both got quiet. I just about froze that night, but it was worth it.

When I was still young enough to be at home all day with Mother, we usually had one or two hungry men come each week and knock on the front door to ask for food. Mother never refused anyone. I carried the plate out to them where they sat in the swing, ate the meal, said thank you, and walked away.

Life was hard for many in the 1930s; however, we kids did not realize it. We had our family, friends, school, and church. Little did we anticipate how much things would change in the 1940s.

The Sherman kids' trio—Cecil with a clarinet, Ruth with a marimba, and Bill with a trombone in 1942.

2
THE FORMATIVE YEARS

The 1940s

In fall 1940, I entered third grade with Mrs. Bethany. E.D. Dunlap was our pastor, and he was always friendly to me. I enjoyed speaking to our pastors and appreciated when they called me by name. Once a year we had the pastor over for Sunday dinner, and I looked forward to those occasions.

When I was in fourth grade, Daddy came home with a trombone. Consequently, I began to play in the Poly Elementary band directed by Mr. Carson. We rehearsed on Thursdays after school. Playing in school assemblies from time to time, we were beginners and sounded like it.

In fact, music was a big part of my siblings' and my life during our school years. Cecil played the clarinet and saxophone. Ruth played the piano, marimba, flute, and bells. And I played the trombone. We were a part of the bands, orchestras, and glee clubs throughout our school days. We also sang in the church choir and ensembles through the years.

One day that fall Mr. Fisher, our principal, appeared in my classroom and told me to come to his office. I was scared because going to the principal's office usually meant you had misbehaved. Instead, he told me my grandfather had fallen in the barn and Mother was coming to pick me up. I was very upset. On the way to the farm Mother drove faster than I had ever seen her drive. Bamaw met us in tears saying, "He's still in the barn. He was gathering eggs and slid over the loose hay. His leg fell through the loft and wedged between the baled hay, and it broke his leg." We rushed out to the barn where the ambulance waited. Several men were trying to pick up Dad Brannon but were sliding so much on the loose hay themselves that they could not lift him. Dad Brannon was hurting badly, which broke my heart to see. Finally, they were able to lift him down from the loft. He spent the next several months at our house recovering. Shortly after this small tragedy struck our family, a much larger tragedy struck the entire nation.

December 7, 1941 was a normal Sunday at our house. We went to Sunday School and worship. Daddy drove to the icehouse, bought twenty-five pounds of ice for homemade ice cream, put it on the front bumper, and drove home. After dinner we climbed into our 1933 Plymouth and drove out to the farm. On the way we stopped at Mr. Hester's house to drop off a Training Union quarterly, a church lesson guide. Mr. Hester came out to the car with tears streaming down his face saying, "John, Annie Mae, have you heard the news? The Japanese have bombed Pearl Harbor and Manila. Our son is stationed in the Philippines, and we haven't heard from him." All of us were in shock. Daddy replied, "Well, this means that we are at war." I really did not know what to make of the whole situation. Daddy drove about fifty miles per hour all the way to the farm. While Dad Brannon and Bamaw did not have electricity, they did have a battery radio. We gathered around the radio for the next few hours along with the rest of the nation. This is how our family learned about America's involvement in World War II.

The next day at school we assembled in the auditorium and listened to the radio as President Roosevelt gave his famous speech to Congress. He began, "Yesterday, December 7, 1941, a date which will live in infamy, the United States of America was suddenly and deliberately attacked by naval and air forces of the Empire of Japan." He concluded by urging Congress to declare war on Japan. Congress concurred with a cheer. As a nine-year-old I wondered what the result of this action would be. We would soon find out.

Life accelerated immediately, and a wave of patriotism swept across the nation. Lines stretched around the block as men volunteered for all branches of the Armed Forces. American industry kicked into overdrive, making planes, guns, ships, tanks, jeeps, and any item necessary for war. War bond drives began with movie stars urging Americans to buy bonds for $18.75. The movie industry began turning out war movies. The nation became united like I have never seen before or since. Pastors spoke from the pulpit urging Americans to rise up and defeat the fascism of Germany, Italy, and Japan. We were inundated with news of the European and Pacific Theaters through newspaper, radio, and the Movietone News at the theater.

On the home front, rationing became the order of the day. The government rationed any item needed for the war effort such as food, gas, and even shoes. Our family had an A card for gasoline rationing, meaning we had an A sticker on our windshield along with a small book of tickets each worth four gallons of gas a week. Our Plymouth got about thirteen to fourteen miles a gallon in town, so we rode the bus and never left Poly. In addition to rationing, we continually had paper drives and scrap iron drives. We even participated in blackouts. Convair built a B-24 heavy bomber plant nine miles west of Fort Worth. When the plant turned out B-24s in late 1942, we had blackouts. If enemy bombers happened to reach Fort Worth, the city needed to be dark. Daddy joined the Texas State Guard, drilling one weekend a month. There were about a thousand men in the Fort Worth Corps, ages thirty-six to fifty-five.

The war took a toll on Poly Baptist as well. Douglas Youngblood, Cecil's Sunday School teacher, and Hall Splawn, a coach at William James Junior High, were both killed in North Africa. Our church had around seventy-five boys serve in the military during those years. Around twenty never returned. Everyone felt the tension of the war.

In 1944 Poly Baptist called Dallas Alford, a student at Southwestern Baptist Theological Seminary, as our music and youth director. He served our church for four years and made a profound impression upon a generation of young people. Cecil and Ruth, who were in high school at the time, joined the church choir along with many of their peers. Dallas was creative, talented, enthusiastic, and dedicated. He created duets, trios, and ensembles for both women and men, and our music ministry became top shelf. He also led after-service fellowships for our young people on Sunday nights. Dallas demonstrated by example who a real Christian was. He made a distinct impression on me. Dallas became the head of the music department at Wayland College in fall 1947. Tragically, he was killed in an automobile wreck in the Texas Panhandle on January 6, 1948. Due in part to his direct influence, the following young people entered Christian ministry: Cecil Sherman, Yandall Woodfin, Dick Wentworth, J.T. Adams, C.A. Roberts, John Wood, Bill Sherman, Ed Crow, Brian Crow, Bill Tolbert, Bryant Tolbert, and Denny Walker. The power of one dedicated life.

Despite the war going on, routines on the home front continued, and as a twelve-year-old I still had life lessons to learn. Cecil shared the milking chores with Daddy. I really wanted to learn to milk, and Daddy consented. In a few weeks I had earned my spurs. Cecil and I took turns milking every other day. He also worked at Ashburn's, an ice cream parlor. One February day he walked in and waved $5 in my face saying, "I'll give you this if you'll do my share of the milking for the rest of the year." I almost broke his arm grabbing the bill out of his hand. I lived to regret my hastiness—all those cold winter mornings and hot summer days. I pleaded my case to Daddy who said, "Son, you made an agreement, and you must keep it!" I learned my lesson and from then on was not so quick to make a decision.

Daddy and Mother both worked during World War II—Daddy at Gulf Oil and Mother at JCPenney. During the summer they would a leave a list of chores for us three kids to do around the house. Ruth was responsible for fixing lunch. My aunt had previously taught her how to make pea salad, and Ruth was good at fixing it. So, guess what? Cecil and I had pea salad in front of our noses almost every day. For the first few weeks it was first class. However, summer lasts for three months. Come the middle of August Cecil and I both made a vow—if we could survive the rest of the summer, we would never again eat pea salad. As the years rolled by and our family gathered for reunions, we never missed having a big laugh about Ruth's pea salad!

Family picture taken in 1948. Cecil and Ruth are in Baylor. Bill is in high school.

Cecil went to Baylor University in Waco, ninety miles south of Fort Worth, in 1945. He drove our 1933 Plymouth with Mother sitting next to him and Jack Robinson sitting next to her. I was in the back seat with all the windows down and three suitcases stacked beside me. (Yes, this was the same Jack Robinson who became an All-American basketball player in 1948, leading the Baylor Bears to the national title game. Later that year he played on the United States Olympic team that won the gold medal in London.) After we dropped Cecil off, Mother cried, and I choked up, too. That night I had the bed all to myself. I looked back and realized what a significant influence Cecil had been on my life. I have always been proud of him and proud to let others know that he was my brother. I have heard some younger siblings say they did not want to follow their older brothers or sisters in school or college, but I followed Cecil and Ruth through grade school, junior high school, high school, Baylor, and Cecil through seminary. What a blessing they were as they opened doors for me.

I hitchhiked down to Baylor from 1947 to 1949 on weekends to watch football games. I stayed with Cecil in the Rutherford House. Pop Rutherford was the barber in the Union Building at Baylor for many years. We ate in Memorial Dining Hall where Cecil and Ruth served tables at lunch and dinner in exchange for free meals. I went to Seventh & James Baptist Church for worship on Sunday mornings and hitchhiked back to Fort Worth on Sunday afternoons. When I came to Baylor as a freshman, I was never homesick. I knew more upperclassmen, thanks to Cecil and Ruth, than I did freshmen. Having my siblings ahead of me in school was both an advantage and a blessing.

A strong influence on my life during the mid-1940s was the Youth Revival Movement whose wellspring was Baylor. Jack Robinson, Charles Wellborn, Bruce McIver, Howard Butt, Frank Boggs, Bo and Dick Baker, Ralph Langley, Warren Hultgren, and Buckner Fanning were on the ground floor of the movement. These young men and others held youth revivals throughout the South for the next fifteen years. Two citywide revivals were held in Fort Worth in the mid- and late 1940s. My initial commitment to special service, as we called it in those days, came at LaGrave Field in Fort Worth when I was in junior high school. God used the Youth Revival Movement to fill our Baptist colleges, universities, and seminaries in the 1940s and 1950s. I later became a part of the movement myself in the 1950s.

In summer 1949 I sold Bibles for the Southwestern Company. I hitchhiked to Nashville, Tennessee, for a week of orientation where we met in the old Maxwell House Hotel. The company assigned my partner, Homer Wheeles, and me to Greene County, Tennessee. We went door to door throughout the county trying to convince tobacco farmers to buy a book or a Bible. This job was a good experience for me, and I met some wonderful people. We stayed all summer in a guest room next to the First Baptist Church. During the second week in August, I hitchhiked back home to begin football practice on August 15 for my senior year at Poly.

High school was a wonderful time. I started attending Poly in fall 1947. Band, books, and sports were my focus, but I did find time to date several girls. My favorite teacher was Patricia Edwards, who taught English and showed a personal interest in me. Perry Sandifer was our band director. He was gifted, loved students, and built the best high school band in town. I enjoyed football, loved track, and was decent in basketball. My junior year our mile relay team won city. My best 100-yard dash time was 10.2 seconds. My senior year our mile relay won city and came in second in state with a 3:30 time. These times do not compare to today; however, this was seventy years ago on a cinder track. My biggest disappointment my senior year was when I broke my leg playing football. I was the tailback in the single-wing formation. We played muscle football with the tailback carrying the ball most plays. With that injury I felt like my chances of playing scholarship football at Baylor had vanished. Still, I looked forward to following Cecil and Ruth to Baylor in fall 1950.

Led by Floyd Chaffin, who came as pastor in 1943, Poly Baptist enjoyed remarkable growth in the years following World War II. (My mother served on the pulpit committee that brought Chaffin from Coleman, Texas.) This growth enabled the congregation to build a new meeting house in 1947. In 1948 Bryant Tolbert became our minister of music. I joined the choir that year and later enjoyed singing in a men's quartet. By the fall of my senior year, Sunday School attendance had climbed to 1700. In 1949 Dr. Woodson Armes came from Seventh & James Baptist Church in Waco, Texas, as our pastor.

When I look back on the eighteen years that I was a member of Poly Baptist, I realize that the folk in that church made a huge impact in shaping my Christian life. My grandfather had been the pastor at Poly from 1920 to 1921. His memorial service was in that church. My parents were Sunday School leaders there for a combined 104 years. Daddy served as a deacon. My siblings and I were baptized in that church. I genuinely feel the words of Paul are appropriate when he wrote, "we are debtors . . ." (Rom 8:12

KJV). I know the Sherman kids were each indebted to our home church. Now Baylor University loomed before me with a surprise waiting in the wings—a blessing of which I had truly dreamed.

3
BAYLOR UNIVERSITY

1950–1952

My life took a fortuitous turn in spring 1950. A postcard came to our house from Cecil, who was now a senior at Baylor University, that read, "Bill, Baylor has a new football coach—George Sauer. He is having high school seniors come during spring training to try out for a scholarship. Why don't you come down and work out with them?" I was excited about the prospect. I had been running track since the first of the year and was in the best shape I had ever been. I weighed 175 pounds. Two days later I was on the field at Baylor. After the workout Coach Sauer brought Johnny Curtis and James Mott over to where Red Donelson and I were standing. They were two of the fastest ball players on the squad. Coach Jack Wilson took all four of us sixty yards up the field where we were to run a sprint so he could get a reading on our speed. I was on edge. He blew the whistle, and I got a good start and won the sprint. I was tickled. But then Coach Sauer said, "Mott, Curtis, you guys were dogging it. Let's run again, and I want you guys to put out!" Coach Wilson moved us back to ninety yards. As we walked back, Mott said, "Billy Don, if you beat me again and come to Baylor, I'm going to haze the dickens out of you." I replied, "James, give me a break; I'm just trying to get a chance to play football." I knew he was just kidding. I had met him through Cecil and watched him play for two years. We ran again, and I won again. In all fairness Mott and Curtis had just worked out in full pads for ninety minutes while I was in shorts and a T-shirt. Coach Sauer thanked us and then asked me to come inside for a conversation. I felt apprehensive. Cecil, who had been standing across the field, came up and asked, "What did he say? What did he say?" Bob Dyal, one of the managers on the team, gave me some good advice. He said, "Billy Don, don't tell Coach Sauer that you are coming to Baylor. If you do, he will simply say that you could walk on. You won't be given a scholarship."

I had mixed feelings when I walked in to talk with Coach Sauer. He said, "Son, where are you going to college?" "Some place where I can play football," I replied. He then asked, "Do you think you can play college football?" "Yes, sir," I replied. He looked to "Uncle Jim" Crow and asked, "What do you think, Jim?" Jim replied, "George, I think we ought to give him full board." Words cannot express the feelings I had in that moment. When I went out to see Cecil, his eyes were as big as teacups. After I told him what had happened, we both went wild!

The summer flew by. I moved into Kokernot Hall on the Baylor campus in September. Wallace Talbert, who had played football with me at Poly, was my roommate. Classes and football workouts began right away. On the first day of workouts, freshmen were on a separate field from the varsity. We were all getting acquainted when Coach Wilson came over to meet the new freshmen. He asked my name and said, "Sherman, with those ears you look like a taxicab coming down the street with both back doors wide open." We all had a good laugh. I have always had big ears.

My freshman year went by in a hurry—meeting new friends was a delight, classes were challenging, and football was demanding. Adjusting to the size of college guys took a while. In high school I was as big as anybody else, but in college the players were bigger and faster and so were the collisions. Freshmen had their own schedule and only played five games. In our first game we rolled over Blinn Junior College. I started at defensive back and played well. In our second game we shut down the Texas A&M freshmen. In the second half of that game, we three defensive backs asked Coach Sam Boyd if we could stay in on offense; he agreed. A coach called a sweep to the left for me to carry the ball, and I ended up in the end zone. I was high as a kite. However, the next time I carried the ball, an opposing player hit me hard on the left shoulder, and I sustained a broken collarbone. My season had ended for the second year in a row.

Singing in the Baylor Religious Hour (BRH) choir was a meaningful experience my freshman year. The BRH was a worship service held on campus in Waco Hall every Wednesday night. Over a thousand students attended. The choir sang, and outstanding speakers shared. BRH established a good atmosphere and helped to reinforce Baylor's Christian mission.

Another activity that I enjoyed was Friday night missions. Each Friday night student teams would go into primarily African American and Latino neighborhoods near campus. These teams would lead a mini-worship service, sing songs, and tell the children about Jesus. We were able to share and get to know the kids, building bridges and relationships.

Singspiration was another popular tradition at Baylor. During Homecoming Week several hundred students would gather in the Drawing Room of the Student Union Building for a time of worship through song. Sitting on the furniture, steps, and floor, we sang choruses, gospel songs, and popular hymns such as "Longing for Jesus," "Turn Your Eyes Upon Jesus," and "I'd Rather Have Jesus." Dick Baker's songs were especially popular. Incredible musical talent was abundant on campus.

I was there when Baylor played and won its first football game in the new Baylor Stadium (later renamed Floyd Casey Stadium) against the University of Houston. Prior to that, the team played its games at the old Municipal Stadium on Dutton Avenue. "Old Muny" could only seat twenty thousand with scores more standing around the fences. The new stadium could seat fifty thousand, counting the end zones. Larry Isbell was the new quarterback. We freshmen scrimmaged the varsity, running the plays of their next opponent each week. Baylor's record was a respectable 7–3 that first season.

One of the best things that happened my freshman year was that I began to date Veta. Ironically, we had met the previous year when I came down to a football game. Cecil and Ruth both worked in Memorial Dining Hall and had taken me there for a meal. They introduced me to scores of girls; consequently, I did not remember all of them. Later, after one of our football workouts, my roommate and I decided to drive out to Latham Springs Baptist Encampment to the pre-school retreat. About three hundred students were there. After the evening service we gathered around the water fountain, and Veta was there. She was friendly and reminded me that we had already met; we reconnected. I thought to myself, "This is a nice girl who possesses both class and looks." However, she was an upperclassman; so, as time went by, I dated various other girls. Finally, in December I asked Veta for a date; and we dated off and on for the rest of the school year.

Baylor's Homecomings—with the parade, the bonfire, and the pep rallies—were special and loads of fun. The week was always abuzz with excitement. And Homecoming meant that basketball season was upon us.

Baylor's basketball team won the Southwest Conference in 1948 and 1950. In both years they advanced to the NCAA Final Four. In 1948 the University of Kentucky beat them for the National Championship. In 1950 Bradley University beat them by two points in the Final Four. Baylor played its home games in Marrs-McLean Gym, which only seated 3,500. Baylor's enrollment was five thousand, so tickets were a scramble. Ralph Johnson was the best player my freshman year. Their record was 8–16 for the year and 3–9 in the conference. Even though 1951 was a rebuilding year, the team was fun to watch.

Baylor was on the quarter system with three quarters in an academic year. Students had three major courses and one elective to attend every day. My first quarter I made two Bs and a C. My elective was football. Cecil really came down on me for not making all As. He was right, yet I was enjoying all the freedom a young person experiences in college. My first year at Baylor was complete.

During summer 1951 I enjoyed two special events. The first was Ruth's marriage to Joel Bruner, a fellow Baylor graduate. Ruth was a wonderful sister. She had always excelled in her grades and her musical gifts and had an especially good voice. She related well to her peers. Joel was enrolling in Southwestern Baptist Theological Seminary, and the couple was headed to Fort Worth.[1]

The other event that I enjoyed that summer was a choir tour with BRH. We sang in churches from Waco to Pensacola, Florida. After each concert one of our ministerial students preached a short sermon. The choir toured on a Greyhound bus accompanied by a van carrying the lights and equipment. Just west of the Florida line, a car struck the van, causing it to roll several times. Thankfully, our two colleagues escaped serious injury although a doctor treated one for a broken wrist. The van was a total loss.

Fall 1951 saw Baylor and Texas A&M picked to win the Southwest Conference in football. I was playing secondary behind Lefty Jones. I was also on the special teams—kickoffs, receiving, and punting. We ended the season with a record of 8-2-1. The Orange Bowl Committee invited us to play Georgia Tech, coached by the one and only Bobby Dodd.

Our experience at the Orange Bowl was special. The Waco Chamber of Commerce gave all the Baylor players new Stetson hats. On the bus ride from the airport to Miami, Florida, we gawked in amazement. Our line coach, Mike Machalsky, said to one of our players, "Charlie Bob, you are a long way from Quanah, Texas, now!" The team roared with laughter. The Orange Bowl Committee provided us with a trip to the dog tracks and the Hialeah Park Racetrack and treated us to a huge banquet. On gameday the fans packed the stands—primarily the Georgia Tech Yellow Jackets fans, as Atlanta, where their campus was located, was closer to Miami than Waco. We dominated the game in the first half, leading 14–7 despite having had a touchdown called back. Georgia Tech rallied in the second half and tied the score.

---

[1]   After SWBTS the couple moved to Magnolia, Arkansas, where Joel took a job as the Baptist Student Union director at Southern State College. Joel eventually left the ministry to join the postal service, and the couple settled in Oklahoma City where they raised their two sons, Woody and Andy. In 1988 Joel divorced Ruth. Providence provided her with another husband, Roger Hamm, and they enjoyed twenty-five years of marriage together. Ruth and Roger loved to travel and did so extensively. Roger passed away in 2019, and Ruth followed in 2020.

In the fourth quarter Larry Isbell, our quarterback, lost his footing and sailed a wobbly pass that Georgia Tech picked off, eventually leading to a Georgia Tech field goal. Georgia Tech won the game. Losing was a bitter pill to swallow. Coach Dodd said at the Copacabana Club that night, "I kinda hesitate to take this trophy, for Baylor beat us in every way today except the scoreboard." Playing in the Orange Bowl was a once-in-a-lifetime experience.

During my sophomore year I lived in Brooks Hall with three other roommates, including Howie Hovde, captain of the basketball team. We later laughed about the fact that Veta had written to both of us during summer 1951, and neither of us knew about it. He dated her several times as well. Veta and I each attended Seventh & James Baptist Church adjacent to campus. This was the year that we became a couple, and I never dated another girl from then on. My classes went well, and I enjoyed Bible courses taught by Rev. Charles Wellborn and Dr. Eddie Dwyer as well as my first history course with Professor Bob Reid.

Veta and I became engaged in spring 1952. I popped the question on campus one evening as we stood by the Armstrong-Browning Library. Although we both agreed that we would not marry until she had finished her degree, I had a good feeling knowing that she would be the one with whom I would spend the rest of my life. Asking Veta to marry me was one of my best decisions.

In March 1952 Jerry Coody and I held a weekend youth revival at the Laird Hill Baptist Church just outside Kilgore in East Texas. Kilgore was the heart of the East Texas oil field—on one city block there were fifty oil derricks—and many members of the congregation worked in the oil fields. Several weeks later Brother V.M. Nipper, the pastor, called and asked if I would be interested in being their summer youth and music director. All the strings seemed to go through the ring, so that is where I spent the summer. Laird Hill provided a wonderful time of learning and serving. Brother Nipper was a delightful man with a keen sense of humor, and his congregation loved him. One Sunday Brother Nipper was preaching on the blessings of being a believer in Christ, and he wanted to focus on how much he believed. He said, "Let me tell you, brother, I would be willing to BET you my . . ." He paused, realizing he was using a gambling term in the sermon. The congregation sat up in the pews, waited a few seconds, and then burst into laughter! Brother Nipper turned red as a beet and then laughed with us. He later said, "Well, if I had just gone on, no one would have paid any attention." I learned a lot that summer. I stayed one month each with three different families. One of the families, the Charlie Pettys, came to our wedding the following summer.

Fall 1952 was a rebuilding year for Baylor football. Our record was 4-4-2. "Almost" was the key word as we lost to Arkansas, Texas, and Rice by a combined eleven points. I enjoyed a decent year in the secondary and led the conference in interceptions with seven.

I had the good fortune of enjoying one of the best plays of my college career in 1952 against TCU at Amon Carter Field in Fort Worth. I was playing cornerback that day. Ronald Clinksdale was the TCU tailback. We knew each other quite well from high school as he had gone to Arlington Heights and we had run track against each other. He was a class young man. In the third quarter Ronald took the snap and ran my way. I took two quick steps toward him and broke back in coverage. He passed the ball, and I picked it off. I knew I could not outrun him to the corner, so I weaved in behind him and picked up several blockers. I weaved in and out and side to side, faking and cutting for fifty-seven yards to the TCU six-yard line. On the next play Allen Jones scored and tied the game. Daddy told me that he was so glad for that play. He worked at the Gulf Oil Corporation where all the folks were big TCU fans. He had a field day with his coworkers on Monday morning.

In school I had a double major in history and religion. Dr. Ralph Lynn was one of the finest professors that I had at Baylor. He not only taught us history, but he also taught us how to analyze and comprehend material. Professor Henry Trantham taught the history of Greece and Rome. He was a Greek scholar and the only Rhodes Scholar ever to serve on the faculty at the time. Professor Bob Reid and Dr. Leonard Duce were also top-flight professors.

4
BAYLOR UNIVERSITY AND JAMAICA

1953–1955

On Wednesday, May 11, 1953, a devastating tornado hit Waco, killing 114 and injuring 597. That afternoon I was working at the track at Municipal Stadium. Weather forecasters had predicted the possibility of storms, and a tornado had struck San Angelo, Texas, earlier that afternoon, killing several people. A few of us walked back toward Brooks Hall together and stood in Mingle-wood Bowl looking at the skies. The heat was stifling. Back to the southwest the clouds were dark and purple, and lightning flashed. All of a sudden, the wind picked up, and several of us ran into the front office of Brooks Hall. Rain and wind came roaring in, and the sky darkened. The wind was blowing so hard that the rain was falling horizontally to the ground. We were staring out the window when Weldon Holley hollered, "Get away from the windows. I think we're in a tornado." He was from Odessa, Texas, and had been in a tornado before. The noise increased, sounding like a freight train overhead. The chaos lasted about six or seven minutes. Suddenly the sun came out, and we all walked outside. About this time the doors opened to the Chow Hall, a frame building near Brooks where all the scholarship athletes ate their meals. We headed in for supper only to find all the lights were out. Looking out the window, we saw Dean Perry running across the softball field, water splashing all around him. He ran into the Chow Hall and screamed, "Men, a terrible tornado has hit down-town Waco. The R.T. Dennis Building [a local department store] has collapsed. People are buried in the rubble. The chief of police has asked all able-bodied men to come and help dig these people out." We were in shock. Everybody jumped up, ran out of the Chow Hall, and headed for town—ten city blocks away. Piling into cars, we were only able to travel two blocks before downed power lines and roofs blocked our way. At that point we abandoned the cars and simply ran to town. We could see the R.T. Dennis Building that had collapsed and covered 5th Street. We ran by the Dr Pepper plant where the north wall lay on the railroad tracks. We climbed through high power lines that covered the tracks. When we finally got to town, it resembled an ant bed. Men were picking up debris everywhere. The center of the city from 5th Street to the courthouse hardly had a building standing. People were digging frantically. The sight was overwhelming. The police told us to call out for the medical folks when we uncovered a victim. We dug until dark when heavy equipment came in from Fort Hood Army Post, and authorities asked all Baylor students to clear out so the Army could take over. We walked back to campus in the dark, as electricity was out in most of south and southwest Waco, including the Baylor campus. I took a shower in the dark. All of us were still in shock. We talked for a while and finally went to sleep around 1:00 a.m. For days the campus was quiet. After about a week, things began to slowly return to a semblance of normal. I had never been afraid of the wind before; however, several months passed before I quit looking to the sky during thunderstorms.

Youth revivals thrived during the late 1940s and 1950s. From 1951 to 1957 I had the privilege of preaching or leading the music in forty-one of them. Most of these were during the summers, yet some were on weekends during the school year. I was aware that some of the invitations may have come because I was a Baylor football player and not because of my outstanding music or preaching ability. My first revival was in Parsons, Kansas. The week went well, and some of the young people made professions of faith. Later several of them came to Baylor as students. In the years that followed I had the privilege of leading revivals in Louisiana, Kansas, Arkansas, and Texas. Needless to say, I had some wonderful experiences and met some great people during those

Ruins of R.T. Dennis Department Store after the Waco tornado, May 11, 1953.

years. One experience comes to mind. I led the music in a revival at Central Baptist Church in Hot Springs, Arkansas, pastored by Dr. Clyde Hart Sr. His youngest son, Clyde Hart Jr., was a senior in high school. He was an outstanding sprinter and had won state in the 100-yard dash the previous year. His dad said, "Bill, I want you to talk to Clyde Jr. He's leaning toward LSU, and I want him to go to Baylor." In the afternoons Clyde Jr. and I worked out together and ran wind sprints. I had pretty good wheels, but I could not keep up with him. He ran a 9.6 100-yard dash while my best time was 10.2. When I came back to Baylor for my senior year in 1953, I saw Clyde Jr. in the Athletic Dining Hall. I was surprised and pleased to see him. He had come to run track for the Green and Gold—Baylor University.

Now we will telescope forward to a Baylor Heritage Club meeting around 2012. The Heritage Club is for Baylor alumni who graduated over fifty years ago. Veta and I had the honor of being co-chairpersons that year. The featured speaker was Clyde Hart Jr., the distinguished track and field coach at Baylor University.

Bill and Veta serving as co-chairpersons for Religious Emphasis at BU in 1953.

Following his presentation was a question-and-answer session in which a participant asked, "Coach, what led you to come to Baylor?" Clyde replied, "I was set to go to LSU, but our church had a youth revival led by two Baylor guys whom I was impressed with. So on a trip out west that summer Dad drove through Waco, and we visited with Coach Wilson. We continued on our trip, and when we stopped in West Texas, I called Coach Wilson and told him I was coming to Baylor." Veta and I were sitting on the front row that morning. When he told that story, I was amazed. I had no earthly idea such was the case. The youth revivals were a catalyst in the spiritual lives of thousands of young people, filling our Baptist universities and seminaries with preachers, missionaries, and Christian educators. God used that movement as a life-changing experience for hundreds of young people and for those of us who had various leadership roles as well.

On August 8, 1953, Veta and I got married at the Poly Baptist Church in Fort Worth. Dr. W.J. Wimpee and Dr. Woodson

Armes officiated the ceremony. Dr. Wimpee was the chaplain at Baylor in those years. He was a mentor to me, providing valued insights when I served as president of the Baptist Student Union that year, as well as a good friend. Dr. Armes had come from Seventh & James Baptist Church in Waco to be Poly's pastor in 1949. Cecil was my best man. Pat Frazier, one of Veta's roommates, was her maid of honor. The wedding was at 8:00 p.m., and all members of the wedding party were in formal attire. The meetinghouse looked lovely with five candelabras with eleven candles in each. There was just one hitch—the meetinghouse at Poly was not air-conditioned. The church ran out of funds when they built the building in 1948. The members decided to finish the fellowship hall instead and add air conditioning in the years to come. The temperature on August 8 was 106 degrees. Cecil and I stood in the foyer waiting for the processional to begin. As we waited, I repeated the words to "Through the Years," the song I was going to sing to Veta as she approached the platform. My cousin Marshall Williamson played the organ. As the "Wedding March" began to play, Cecil and I took our places at the front. The groomsmen and bridesmaids came forward to take their places, the organ swelled into "Here Comes the Bride," and Veta and her dad marched down the aisle. They paused at the front while I sang "Through the Years." I marvel that those words so aptly describe how our lives have blended. One humorous incident took place during the ceremony. The meetinghouse was quite warm, and I was perspiring, as were others. As Dr. Wimpee said the vow to me, a trickle of perspiration rolled down my forehead and simply hung onto the tip of my nose. I wanted to gently shake my head; however, I feared onlookers might think I was saying "no" to the vow. So I waited, and the drop eventually fell on its own. The salvation of the circumstance was that the fellowship hall, where we were holding the reception, was air-conditioned. We laughed, for as everyone entered the cool hall, they sighed in relief!

Veta and I went to New Mexico and Colorado for our honeymoon. En route across West Texas we stopped for gas. I bounced out and walked around the car and opened the door for Veta.

Some folks who were sitting out in front of the station laughed, and one lady commented, "You can tell they haven't been married long. He still opens the door for her." We all had a good laugh. On Sunday night we worshipped with First Baptist Church, Hobbs, New Mexico. As we left the church, we shook hands with the pastor. He said, "You all are new faces." For seventeen months I had introduced Veta as my fiancée; this was the first time to introduce her as my wife. I promptly said, "Yes, I am Bill Sherman; and this is my wife, Veta Cole." That took a bit of explaining, though we have laughed about the story through the years.

We visited Carlsbad Caverns, Mount Evans, Pikes Peak, and Estes Park. The mountains of Colorado were spectacular. We ended our trip at the Royal Gorge. Ten days later we came home, having driven 2,700 miles in our new 1953 Plymouth.

After those cool days in Colorado, we moved to Waco in 100-degree temperatures. Veta had a teaching job at Sul Ross Elementary School just a few blocks from Baylor's campus. I was facing two-a-day workouts for my senior year with the football team. We moved into the Homettes, which were used for married student housing and located where North Russell Hall stands today. These were prefab buildings that had been moved from Connally Air Force Base just north of Waco. Our rent was $25 a month.

As school cranked back up, so did college football. Baylor and Texas were favorites to win the conference. A rule change took place in the NCAA that year that ended free substitutions. Each player had to play both offense and defense. Our first game was University of California at Berkeley. Cotton Davidson was our quarterback. Their quarterback was Paul Larson, who led the nation in offense in 1952. We flew to Berkeley, where the papers did not give us a chance. In fact, most sportswriters did not even know where Baylor was located. At the end of the game the score was Baylor 25, California 0. We flew to Miami, Florida, two weeks later and beat the University of Miami 21–13. By now polls ranked us in the top ten in the nation. After winning our next four games, we moved up to third in the nation. Next, we traveled to Austin, Texas, to play a knock-down-drag-out game against the

Picture taken in 1953 at Baylor Stadium after a Baylor victory over SMU.

University of Texas. When the smoke cleared, the score was Texas 21, Baylor 20; and we fell to seventh in the national rankings. Our entire team was down. Coach Sauer was not a personable man. He was aloof and distant and never got close to his players. He was, without a doubt, the man in charge, and no one would cross him. The team was full of dissension over Sauer's use of players. This tension cost us our next game. The University of Houston beat us 37–7 in Waco. We beat SMU in Waco, but lost to Rice in Houston, costing us the conference championship. Our season record was 7–3. I have often thought what might have happened if we had a coach who could inspire and motivate his players.

Overall, my senior year was a good experience. Jerry Coody and I alternated at left halfback. I ended up with five interceptions for the season. One embarrassing play happened against TCU. Ernest Newman, a Fort Worth guy I had played against in high school, fielded Baylor's punt. I was closing in for the tackle right in front of the TCU bench. As I was about to lay one on Newman, he juked. I flew right past him and knocked Coach Abe Martin sprawling. Embarrassed and afraid I had hurt him, I jumped up and went over to pick him up. He said, "Sherman, you jarred my ancestors." I apologized and jogged back to the field, greatly relieved that he was not hurt.

Though my senior season did not end as I would have liked, I am deeply appreciative for my football experience at Baylor and am indebted to Coach Sauer. He gave me a shot—a shot that paid for my college education—when other coaches simply asked me to walk on. When you look at the larger picture in life, sports are not all that important; however, they are enjoyable, and you meet a ton of folks who become lifelong friends. Football was truly an experience that fulfilled a teenage boy's dream and playing for Baylor University was both an honor and a thrill. Veta and I (until COVID) have missed only one Baylor Homecoming football game since 1949. That year we were with our oldest son, Donny, who was in treatment for melanoma at MD Anderson in Houston. I will share more on that later.

My senior classes at Baylor went well. I particularly enjoyed those with Dr. Bernard Ramm in religion, Dr. Ralph Lynn and Professor Bob Reid in history, and Professor Henry Trantham in Greek. Veta likewise enjoyed her class with the fourth grade at Sul Ross Elementary. Time and time again she would come home with funny stories. Sul Ross was in an old neighborhood in Waco that served a wide variety of students.

One student, Roger, had a father who was a Pentecostal preacher. Roger had a keen sense of humor. At the lunch table Veta asked little Peter Maciel to drink his milk. She said, "If you want to grow up and be an athlete like those at Baylor, you must drink your milk." Roger said, "Mrs. Sherman, I know about them athletes. My brother has 'em on his feet." Another time the class had just sung "America the Beautiful," and Veta said, "Now, boys and girls, do you understand the meaning of 'and crown thy good with brotherhood'?" One sweet girl replied, "I know,

Mrs. Sherman. The Brotherhood is a men's organization in our church." Roger added, "Mrs. Sherman, I know Brother Hood. He's a member of my daddy's church." Needless to say, Veta had a stimulating year at Sul Ross.

After taking a Masters in Divinity from Southwestern Seminary, Cecil and Dot married on December 27, 1953 and moved to New Jersey for Cecil to complete a Masters in Theology at Princeton. They subsequently returned to Southwestern for Cecil to begin his doctoral studies.[1]

In spring 1954 I had a call from Dr. Wimpee. He had received a phone call from Mr. Lentz, a deacon from Malone Baptist Church. They needed a pastor and wondered if Dr. Wimpee could recommend someone. I did not know where Malone was, but I found out that it was a small farming community of two hundred people about seven miles north of Hubbard, Texas. I learned that I was preaching in the Malone Baptist Church the next Sunday. Veta and I had been the directors of the freshman Sunday School department at Seventh & James where there were about 250 freshmen in attendance each Sunday. The next Sunday I was preaching to nineteen folks at Malone. I must say that it was an adjustment. After the service the members asked Veta and me to stand on the front porch while they had a business meeting. That was the beginning of four happy years of serving as their pastor. There were forty-one members on the roll, twelve of whom were unable to attend services due to health issues. We commuted out each Sunday and spent the day, eating Sunday dinner with a different family each week. The salary was $25 a Sunday. That is how my formal ministry began. The pastorate at Malone was a good experience for me, and the congregation became family. This was our Sunday pattern for two years at Baylor and two years

---

[1] After receiving his doctorate in 1956, Cecil was called to First Baptist Church, Chamblee, Georgia, where his daughter, Eugenia, was born. The young family returned to Texas for a brief stint from 1960 to 1964 for Cecil to serve as pastor of First Baptist Church, College Station and to work for the Baptist General Convention of Texas in campus ministries. In 1964 Cecil was called to First Baptist Church, Asheville, North Carolina, where he served for the next twenty years.

at Southwestern Seminary. I must say that those gracious people put up with some poor sermons, but they were patient and loving. Leaving them was hard.

Graduation took place at Baylor Stadium on a Sunday evening in spring 1954. The four years had gone by in a hurry. To put on the cap and gown and realize that there would be no more term themes or tests to face was a relief. Dr. W.R. White was Baylor's president at the time. When the announcer called my name, I gladly walked across the platform and shook Dr. White's hand. He said, "Congratulations, Billy Don, and may the best be yours." I had a barrel of memories as I looked across the stadium that night—most of them were good ones.

Jamaica

After graduation, Dr. Wimpee asked Veta and me if we would like to serve as summer missionaries to Jamaica in June. That was like asking if there was a cow in Texas; we were delighted to go to Jamaica. He explained that each participating state was sending two students to work in Vacation Bible Schools (VBS). We were excited about the prospect. We came down to earth quickly the next week, however, when Dr. Wimpee said, "Bill and Veta, there has been a mix-up. Texas has already chosen its two students. However, Dr. Howard shared that they would welcome you to the group if you can raise $800 in the next two weeks." Veta's salary for nine months teaching school was $2,300. So, $800 was one third of her total salary. We quickly got to work. We contacted some Waco folks who gave some modest funds. I wrote to a number of churches where I had held youth revivals in the past several years. We waited, and we prayed. An amazing feat happened. In two weeks' time, over $1,200 came in the mail. We were stunned. The day before we left, Veta and I went to the farm to tell Dad Brannon and Bamaw goodbye. With genuine excitement I told them the story. Bamaw replied, "Why are you so surprised? God just did what He told us He would do." When I thought about it, I realized that Bamaw was on target. Serving that summer in Jamaica was God's plan for us.

The other couples from New Mexico, Texas, Oklahoma, and Arkansas gathered in Dallas. We boarded a Greyhound bus and rode to Montgomery, Alabama. The next morning, we boarded the bus again and rode nineteen hours to Miami, Florida. That bus ride was a hoot! We occupied seats in the middle of the bus on either side and told jokes and sang choruses. In Georgia some Royal Ambassadors (RAs) boarded the bus going to RA camp. We visited with them and told jokes. We finally arrived in Miami— ready to stand up for a while.

We stayed in Miami for three days while William Hall Preston from the Student Union Department of the Sunday School Board in Nashville, Tennessee, led an orientation. Then we boarded the plane for Kingston, Jamaica. Ironically, the Southern Baptist missionaries who worked in harmony with the Jamaica Baptist Union were C.W. and Avis McCullough. C.W. had been Veta's pastor when she was a child in Rochelle, Texas, and he was a student at Howard Payne. In fact, he baptized her in a stock tank when she made her commitment to Christ. C.W. met our group at the airport where a bus was waiting to take us into town. After we had stacked the luggage on top of the bus, C.W. said to Veta and me, "You all ride with me, and we will follow the bus." A traffic light stopped our car, and the bus went on ahead. When we caught up you would not believe what we saw. A large, iron I-beam held up a low bridge for the train tracks. The road went under this low I-beam. When the bus drove under this bridge, the stacked suitcases, which did not make clearance, crashed into the street below. As we drove up, we saw the entire contents of our suitcases littering the road, the trees, and the ditches. The driver was beside himself. Students were walking around holding up pants, underwear, shirts—you name it—asking, "Is this yours?" We just had to laugh. We gathered everything up in about forty-five minutes and continued to the missionaries' house. This was our first day in Jamaica.

The next day the McCulloughs shared some insights that would help us as we related to the Jamaicans. That evening we worshipped in the largest Baptist church in Kingston. We sang these words, "In Christ there is no east or west, in Him no south or north; But one great fellowship of love throughout the whole wide earth." The service was a meaningful and uplifting way to begin the summer.

The next day, Saturday, teams of four moved throughout the island to the churches in which they would lead VBS the following week. C.W. said, "Bill, Veta, I have a special assignment for you. Rev. O.T. Johnson pastors a church on the north coast in Oracabessa. He is in Belize for six weeks doing mission work for the Jamaica Baptist Union. I want you to live in the manse (parsonage) on a bluff overlooking the Caribbean Sea and pastor his church until he returns." He drove us over that day. I preached the next day and met the people, who were quite friendly. Since the British ruled Jamaica for years, the Anglicans had highly influenced the worship services. The church used a divided chancel, with the lower platform for music and an elevated loft for preaching. I asked the head deacon if I could simply preach from the platform, and he agreed. I preached as best I could, and the folk were kind to listen. After a few Sundays, a warm fellowship developed.

We held our VBS the second week that we were there with Billy Cooper from Louisiana and Jeannie Rudolph from my home church at Poly rounding out our team. Children, young people, and adults filled the church as we marched behind the flags into the meetinghouse while the organ played. Everyone had a big smile on his face wondering what would happen next. We sang "Everybody Ought to Know" as the chandeliers swayed. I led the teenagers; however, we had as many adults as we had youth because Oracabessa was a banana port town.

Once a week a huge freighter, owned by the British Fruit Company, came down for a load of bananas. Farmers brought bananas on carts, trucks, and even bicycles to sell. Carriers picked a stem of bananas about four feet tall, placed it on their heads, ran to a dipping vat and dipped the stem in to ward off varmints, and ran down the dock to large rowboats where workers stacked the stems into a huge pyramid. Workers formed a line, as in a bucket brigade, as they passed each stem. The company paid the carriers by how many stems they carried. Once the carriers finished loading the boat, men rowed it out to the waiting ship. The whole procedure usually began around 10:00 a.m. and lasted about twelve hours. When they finished, the workers lay down on the spot and slept a sleep of death. This is why so many adults came to VBS—there was not any paid labor in Oracabessa except on banana day.

The VBS week was a delight. We became better acquainted with the folk in the town, and worship attendance increased on Sundays. One Friday night after the commencement service, Veta and I were at the parsonage listening to the WFAA Texaco Star Reporter news from Dallas, Texas, when a seventeen-year-old young man named Vinston Clementson walked up onto the front porch. He had been in my class in VBS. When Mrs. Johnson, the housekeeper, saw him, she sprang out of her chair and ran across the room saying, "You can't come in here. You are a sinful man." Veta and I were stunned. He replied, "Please, ma'am, I would like to speak to one of the students." She responded, "Not in here!" I stood up and said, "I'll talk to you, Vinston." She again said, "Not in here." I said, "No problem, I'll go out there." Vinny and I walked down the bluff and sat down on a big boulder on the shore of the Caribbean. As the breeze blew and the waves rolled in and out, I said, "Vinny, I enjoyed having you in my class this week. What would you like to talk about?" He replied, "I have tried all the ways of my friends and have not found satisfaction. I have seen something in you students this week that I would like to have in my life. Would you tell me what it is and how I can get it?" I responded, "Vinny, have you ever met Jesus Christ? He is God's Son, and He came to earth to save us from our sins. He died on the cross to pay the penalty of our sins. If you will simply confess and invite him into your heart, He will forgive you, give you a reason to live, and give you the power to cope with life." He said, "I am ready." I replied, "Vinny, I'm going to pray a prayer, and when I finish, you tell the Lord how you feel and that you are ready to invite Christ into your life." I prayed, then he prayed. I remember his smile when he finished the prayer. He said, "I feel like a load has been lifted off my shoulders." I told him that I would be preaching in the church house on Sunday and asked him if he would come and profess his faith before the congregation. He said, "Yes, but I don't have any shoes." I gave him my loafers that were a little big for him, but he smiled. As we walked up the hill together, he said, "I'm going to ride my bicycle to Kingston and tell my daddy what I've done, but I'll be back on Sunday." Sure enough he was, sitting on the back row of church. When I extended the invitation, he came forward. I welcomed him, and he asked to speak to the congregation. After the invitation closed, I explained to them what happened on Friday night and told them that Vinston wished to say a word. He stood up and said, "You all know me. I am not the same man that you used to know. Last Friday evening I invited Jesus into my heart, and He has changed me." I stood up and said, "I'm sure that all of us will want to surround Vinston with acceptance and encouragement. If you feel this way, would you please vote to accept him into the church." About half of the people responded. Vinny stood at the front, and a number of people came to welcome him. We had the benediction, and I went to the back door to shake hands with the folks. Most accepted Vinston's decision; however, one man came by me and dressed me down. He said, "Preacher, you don't know this young man. Just give him a week, and he'll be back in the brothel." I told him that our role as a church was to accept and encourage. Well, a week later Vinston was riding his bicycle up to Bog Walk and helping me with the young people in VBS. Later, Vinston went to the seminary in Kingston and then became one of the leading pastors in the Jamaica Baptist Union.

Our third week in Jamaica we led a VBS four miles into the interior of the island at a community called Oxford, one of four churches in Rev. Johnston's circuit. Oxford was a poor area where the Jamaicans worked for British landlords raising bananas. One house had an extra bedroom, so Veta and Jeannie stayed there. Billy Cooper and I slept on the benches in the church house. Builders had engineered the church onto the side of a mountain. The entrance was on the road, but the rest of the building was on stilts about fifteen to eighteen feet tall. The first day of VBS children filled the building. The church had a pump organ, and one morning as we were singing the anthem, I noticed a terrible discord—a donkey had stepped just inside the door and was braying to the beat of the band.

The summer in Jamaica really brought home to me the many inequities that exist in our world. For our first breakfast in Oracabessa, we had bananas and slices of pineapple. That was all. For lunch, after leading young people all morning in VBS, we had a glass of tea and three crackers. I waited to see what was next—that was it. For supper, we had a modest meal of vegetables, bread, and bananas. The Jamaicans only ate two meals a day. I weighed 192 pounds when we went to Jamaica, and I returned home weighing 167 pounds. When Veta and I walked into a grocery store back in Miami, we marveled at all the food. The things we take for granted.

I had always felt that you could make something of yourself if you tried. In Jamaica that was not the case. The citizens had few opportunities for work, and the pay was modest at best. If we told a mother how cute her son was, she would reply, "You like him? You may have him." Veta and I came back with a new sense of appreciation for the privileges and opportunities that we enjoy as citizens of the United States.

In fall 1954 Veta and I returned to Baylor for me to pursue a master's degree in history. I continued to serve the church at Malone, and Veta taught at Bell's Hill Elementary. We lived in an apartment on South 10th Street owned by Pearl and Earle Bryan. We had an enjoyable year filled with events at Baylor, school, and church. The following summer was packed with youth revivals again.

Family picture with spouses and first grandson, 1955.

5
SEMINARY AND FIRST BAPTIST, BONHAM, TEXAS

1955–1959

Southwestern Baptist Theological Seminary

We moved to Fort Worth, Texas, in fall 1955, and I entered Southwestern Baptist Theological Seminary to pursue a degree in theology. Veta and I both felt a call to overseas Christian missions. Southwestern was not new ground as I had grown up in Fort Worth. Professors W.T. Connor, T.B. Maston, and Jesse Northcutt had filled the pulpit in my home church for years. When I enrolled at Southwestern, I was entering an entirely different learning experience from Baylor. The trappings of college life were no longer present to distract me from my goal. We were there to sharpen our gifts, and the professors expected us to study. Any form of ministry must have a discipline to it, and seminary is the last opportunity to create a proper study pattern. Thankfully, most students adopted a redemptive pattern. I enjoyed my seminary experience and recognized that the hard work I was putting in was worth that extra effort.

In fall 1956 Baylor had one of the finest football teams around. Doyle Traylor, Bobby Jones, Bill Glass, Delbert Shofner, and Larry Hickman, to name a few, were some of the best players, not only in the conference, but in the nation as well. At the end of the season, the Sugar Bowl Committee invited Baylor and the University of Tennessee to play. I was taking a class with Dr. T.B. Maston in Christian ethics at the time. He had spoken on many occasions at Poly, my home church, when I was growing up. He was also a native Tennessean who had played football at Carson-Newman Baptist College in Jefferson City, Tennessee. Before class one late December day, Dr. Maston said, "Billy Don, I think your Baylor Bears are in over their heads in the Sugar Bowl. Tennessee is ranked second in the nation, and their tailback, Johnny Majors, is going to run the ball down Baylor's throat." He was aware that I had played for Baylor. I responded, "Dr. Maston, I scrimmaged against those Baylor players when they were freshmen in 1953. I can assure you that they will give a good account of themselves." He smiled and replied, "That is an expression of hope." The entire class, about half of whom were Baylor graduates, was taking this conversation in. I countered, "Dr. Maston, since this is an ethics class, wagering would not be proper; however, I'll suggest an arrangement. If Tennessee wins, I'll write an extra paper for you; if the Bears win, I'll get a free cut." He chuckled and replied, "I'll accept that arrangement." The Sugar Bowl was a knock-down-drag-out. Baylor dominated the first half and led 6–0. Tennessee scored in the second half to bring the score to 7–6. In the fourth quarter Baylor recovered a fumble inside the Tennessee fifteen-yard line. Baylor punched the ball in and went ahead 13–7. The final score was Baylor 13, Tennessee 7.

I had never worn my Baylor letter jacket to class; however, as the game ended, I turned to Veta and said, "Get my letter jacket out of the trunk; I'm wearing it tomorrow." When I walked into class, all the Baylor graduates laughed and cheered. In jest I said, "Fellas, did you all know I played ball at Baylor?" When Dr. Maston came in I did not say a word. He died laughing and said, "Okay. Go on." I responded, "No, I'm just glad the Bears pulled the game out." He graciously responded, "Baylor deserved to win."

The Southwestern years were meaningful, though life was a scramble. Veta secured a teaching job at Carter Park Elementary School, and we continued to serve at the church in Malone. The church had two deacons, and one of them, Louie Lentz died that year. His was the first funeral that I ever conducted.

I particularly enjoyed Dr. Jesse Northcutt's preaching classes, as I certainly needed the help. Dr. John Newport's classes in philosophy of religion were informative. Dr. Robert Baker taught challenging church history courses. Dr. A. Donald Bell and Dr.

Othal Feather were two professors in the religious education school who gave helpful and practical ideas in Christian education. Dr. J. Howard Williams was the president of Southwestern in those years. He gave excellent leadership to the school, growing it to the largest of the six Southern Baptist seminaries in the 1950s. I am truly indebted to the Southwestern professors who mentored and shaped my ministry.

An interesting side light took place while I was at Southwestern. There was a tradition that Southwestern and TCU played an annual touch-pass football game every year for bragging rights. This involved any seminary student and the freshman football players from TCU. There were 1,700 students at Southwestern then. When we started counting noses, there were lettermen from Baylor, Hardin-Simmons, Oklahoma, Auburn, Texas A&M, Texas, and a host of smaller colleges. The game was eight on eight—five linemen and three in the backfield. We chose Bill "Cozy" Cozart, who had never played a down of football in his life, as our coach. He was five and a half feet tall and weighed about 130 pounds, but he had a heart for the game. We journeyed over to the intramural field at TCU. Ray Vickery, a former track athlete at Baylor, was our quarterback. TCU was confident they would send the preacher boys home with red faces. The game started out civil enough; but as time went on, it became extremely rough, and we were not in pads. In fact, that game turned out to be one of the roughest games I have ever played in. We beat them, and they were ticked! As we walked off the field, the TCU player coach said, "You guys only won because our best players were in lab this afternoon." Cozart responded, "Bring them on, we'll play you again." Several of us were limping off the field behind them listening to their conversation. I thought, "Good gosh, they will round up some varsity guys and kill us." I intercepted Cozy and said, "Bill, do you realize what those guys will do? They're going to get some varsity guys and drill us." He said, "Sherm, you guys can beat their best guys." The next week we were back at TCU where the game had been moved to Amon Carter Stadium, TCU's home field. We kicked off. TCU did not huddle but lined up on the ball and snapped it while we were in disarray. Their backs came running elbow to elbow right at me. I thought, "Good gosh, this isn't tackle football." That was the opener, and the game went downhill from there! However, at the end of the war, we beat them—again! TCU could hardly believe it. The next year they reneged, and the tradition ended.

In spring 1956 I began working at Convair, nine miles west of Fort Worth, on the swing shift. During World War II Convair made B-24s. Now the plant was making supersonic jets, bombers, and fighters. Working from 3:45 p.m. to 12:15 a.m. enabled me to continue my seminary work and take over the income for our family. Veta had already taught school for three years. We wanted to have children before we were eligible for Social Security. The arrangement was a good one, though something of a scramble. I was in a carpool with five other seminarians who also worked at Convair, which meant I drove every sixth week. Stewardship of time was a must. I continued to take a full load at seminary, work forty hours a week at Convair, and pastor at Malone on Sundays. Those two Southwestern years were probably the busiest and most challenging of my life.

Working at Convair was quite an experience. I learned to drill and shoot rivets, putting the F-104 fighter planes together. Since I was coming in as a green employee, management placed me with a partner, an A-man. I was a B-man. Essentially the A-man tells you what is going on and what to do. My A-man was Red Bumpass, a believing Christian from Weatherford, just up the road. We worked happily together for almost two years, which allowed Veta and me to begin our family. In addition, we moved to a nice rental house on Merida Avenue near Southwestern.

In 1956, we learned that Veta was pregnant. Billy Don Jr. was born on March 9, 1957, at St. Joseph Hospital in Fort Worth. We called him Donny. I went down the hall to see him where the hospital had lined the cribs up next to a viewing window. A lady just a step away said, "Look at this cute little boy. He sure does have big ears." I must say that tested my patience. Our life now had a new orbit. Both of us were tickled pink to be parents, and

Donny was a joy from day one. Veta was a great mother from the beginning. Fortunately, I did not have classes on Mondays, enabling me to have some time as a father and husband. Both sets of parents lived in Fort Worth, which was so helpful in those busy years. Veta's mother was a wonderful source of knowledge and advice. Time passed quickly for us.

First Baptist Church, Bonham, Texas: 1957–1959

While we were attending Baylor Homecoming in 1957, Jack Carson, pastor of First Baptist, Bonham, Texas, approached us and asked, "Bill, Veta, why don't you all come and be my music and youth director. We would make a good team; I think we would be a winning combination." Jack was in Veta's class at Baylor and had been a cheerleader. I was not a music major, nor was I going into church education. However, I had sung in choirs and quartets and had played a trombone for years. We had both grown up in Baptist churches and had been fully involved in most phases of ministry. We thought about it, prayed about it, and ended up moving to Bonham in late fall 1957.

Bonham was a town of seven thousand folks where everyone knew each other. It was also the home of Sam Rayburn, the Speaker of the House of Representatives in Washington, D.C. Mr. Sam's house was just west of town on Highway 82. He enjoyed sitting on his front porch where half the county would come and talk to him. Bonham was Americana.

The church was in a building program. They had razed all their facilities and were in the midst of building everything new—educational space and a meeting house. Sunday morning worship was in the town movie theater while Sunday night worship was in the old Chevrolet facility. Ralph Buffington, out of Houston, Texas, was the architect. The arrangement was a challenge, but everyone had a good spirit about it. I commuted one hundred miles down to Southwestern every Tuesday morning, attended class, and spent the night with my parents. On Wednesday I attended class and drove the one hundred miles back to Bonham for prayer meeting and choir practice. On Thursday and Friday, I repeated the pattern. Saturday through Monday I remained in Bonham. I was on the go!

Ministry during those two years was a ton of fun. We plugged into the town and got to know the people, and they became family. I led the youth choir and church choirs. Several young people were on the high school football team, and I worked out with them. The coach was M.B. Nelson, a model coach and Christian. He had more influence on those young people than any of us church workers. He came up to me the first Sunday, put his arm around me, and said, "Bill, I've worked with young people a long time. They will either be as good or as bad as you let them." He was as right as rain!

The original church building, built in the early 1900s, was the largest meetinghouse in North Texas. Unfortunately, it was built on a splatter foundation with no steel reinforcement. Over the years the foundation began to give way, and the walls were leaning out. Authorities declared the structure unsafe, thus the reason for an entire new facility. When we finally entered the new buildings, we celebrated! The facilities were lovely and made our work easier.

I finished my basic seminary degree in spring 1958. The church gave me a new Sunday suit. I began my graduate work in Christian ethics in fall 1958. The work was intense and demanding but enjoyable. The trick of balancing seminary work, church work, and family life was always a challenge. When I look back, I sometimes wonder how it all fit together. Donny was growing and was the apple of our eyes. No matter how pressed I was, I always had time for Veta and him. My work at First Baptist, Bonham was going well. We had a quality choir, and the young people and adults were enjoyable. The year 1958 flew by. Little did we know that a new chapter was about to unfold in our lives.

6
TWO FINE CHURCHES—McKINNEY, TEXAS AND STILLWATER, OKLAHOMA

1959–1967

First Baptist, McKinney, Texas: 1959–1963

Out of the clear blue one evening we received a telephone call from a gentleman in McKinney, Texas. McKinney, the county seat of Collin County, was located thirty miles north of Dallas with a population of fourteen thousand. Sam Hill, chairman of the search committee at First Baptist Church, was looking for an associate staff member who could wear three hats—music, education, and youth. We had an amiable conversation that led to further talks. We were happy in Bonham, and the people were so gracious. We did not have a reason to leave, yet Veta and I wanted to be open to where God might be leading us. After careful deliberation we felt led to move to McKinney. I was in my second year of postgraduate work in Christian ethics, and McKinney graciously permitted me to continue in this endeavor. Fortunately, the drive to Southwestern was now only fifty miles instead of one hundred. We moved in fall 1959.

Our early days in McKinney were a time of adjustment. Dr. Charles Myers, the pastor, was so gracious. He was a graduate of Baylor as well as Southwestern Seminary and was one of the first to receive a doctorate in ethics at Southwestern in the 1940s. Our salary was $5,200 a year. The church building was one block from the city square. I focused on building up the church choir, meeting the teenagers, and working with the pastor in all phases of church life. I also led the graded choirs. Attendance in Sunday School was just over four hundred. We enjoyed meeting the church people, settling into our home, and getting active in our new community. Life was busy.

In many ways Bonham and McKinney were like life in a Norman Rockwell painting. There was one high school. Everybody knew each other, and church and school activities served as the pulse of the town. We took in all the football games. McKinney High School was a powerhouse in Division 3A. Charles Qualls, the head coach, was a deacon in our church. We became very close friends. Interestingly, his wife, Joan, was a graduate of Poly High School in Fort Worth just a year ahead of me.

Our youth group grew, and the youth choir filled the choir loft every Sunday evening. Each summer I took several carloads of young people and teachers to Glorieta Baptist Assembly in northern New Mexico. The trip was tons of fun and a refreshing break for everyone. Glorieta was also a time of spiritual renewal. About this time the stork visited our marriage, and our daughter, Debbie, was born in December 1959. We were overjoyed and delighted to welcome her into our home. Donny was almost three years old.

In 1961 Dr. Charles Myers accepted the call to First Baptist Church, McAlester, Oklahoma. He had served FBC, McKinney for over twenty years. The folk appreciated his contributions and wished him well. Later that summer the church called Dr. Bailey Stone as pastor. Veta and I had been at Baylor with Bailey and knew him as a class act. We served together for the next two years. He was a great people person and well-received by the church. We frequently went out and played touch-pass football with our youth.

I finished my course work for the Christian ethics degree in 1962, and the next hurdle was the oral examination. In the oral examination, four professors probe and question a ThD candidate for about two hours over all his coursework from the past two years—a formidable hurdle to jump. At the end of the session the professors vote as to whether the candidate has passed. Needless to say, orals get your attention and catch you up on your prayer life, and I blocked off several days for preparation. I loved playing with our kids; however, when crunch time came, I sat at a card table for several hours at a time and asked the kids not to bother Daddy. I hoped they would understand. One day I went in the room to study, told the kids not to come in, and shut the door. Things were calm for about forty-five minutes before I heard Deb's voice outside the door asking to come in. I reminded her of my situation. All was quiet for a minute. Then she pushed open the door in tears and asked, "Daddy, can I get a hug?" She melted my old, cold heart. I opened my arms, and she gleefully came and jumped into them. I can get misty-eyed just remembering the story.

Finally, the time came for my orals. Four professors sat before me. For Christian ethics, Dr. Maston and Dr. Scudder posed the questions. For my minors, Dr. Bill Hendricks in theology and Dr. Jesse Northcutt in preaching attended. Each was gracious but thorough. When a professor posed a question and my response was on target, he would interrupt and jump to another subject. This approach enabled him to cover a wider scope of material. Yes, I was nervous. Dr. Maston, speaking for all four men, assured me that each was my friend, but they needed to ensure that the questions and responses covered the entire body of material. The session went well until Dr. Hendricks challenged one of my answers concerning love as the basis of rightful behavior in 1 John 4. Dr. Maston had shared in seminars that our love for God is expressed and proven by ethical behavior. Consequently, I stood my ground. Dr. Maston encouraged me, saying, "Tell him, Billy Don!" That moment was the only time in the two-hour period that things got a bit tense. Thankfully, the four professors voted that I passed muster.

Still Veta and I both felt that our calling in ministry was in overseas missions. Dr. Henry Goerner, an area secretary at the Foreign Mission Board of the Southern Baptist Convention (SBC), visited Southwestern that fall. We made an appointment to see him. Since I had finished my coursework and orals, we asked him about the possibility of being appointed now and completing my dissertation on our first furlough from the mission field. He replied that the Mission Board had a guideline against this. I shared with him that there were two missionaries in my seminars who were doing just what I had asked about; could Veta and I not do the same? He was caught off guard, and we were confused. He said that he would look into the situation, and that ended the conversation. We returned home to McKinney. I had finished all my education except for my dissertation. We loved the work at McKinney but did not feel this ministry was our calling. The Lord sent us a sign before the week was over in the form of another phone call.

University Heights Baptist Church, Stillwater, Oklahoma: 1963–1967

On a Thursday night in mid-November 1963, Veta and I were getting ready to watch several guys in our youth group play a B-team football game when the phone rang. A voice on the other end of the line said, "Bill, you don't know me. My name is Ed Lemons, and I hope this telephone call will be the beginning of a long relationship with you and your family." He continued, "I am the chairman of the pulpit committee for University Heights Baptist Church in Stillwater, Oklahoma. We need a pastor who will challenge our students at Oklahoma State University (OSU) to go all out for Christ. Your brother preached for us last Sunday, and he recommended that I call you. He felt that you and your wife might just fit the bill for our church." This call was the beginning of four years of an exciting ministry in a college church. After visiting with Ed for about twenty minutes, we told him that we would talk about his request, pray for the Lord's guidance, and get back with him in a few days. First, we had to discuss if this was a door that the Lord was opening for us—was missions or the pastorate what God had in mind for our lives? We genuinely prayed for a sense of direction. We concluded that our field of ministry was to the world. But where would that take us? We had always felt that God works through open and closed doors. We would let this be our guide to the direction we should take. This door had opened—should we walk through? We decided to go and see. We talked with the church folks in McKinney and Stillwater and shared our feelings. Both were supportive. The holiday season delayed the timing. We had been working on the Christmas music and felt that we needed to carry on where we were through the end of the year. Communication lines remained open while we continued to serve in McKinney through December.

During the latter part of January, I went to Stillwater to preach as a supply for one Sunday. This was not in view of a call but for each side to get a feel for the situation. Veta was expecting our third child and was seven months along. She stayed home in light of the circumstances. The church desperately needed leadership as the former pastor had not reached out to the people. I preached from Paul's text, "For I determined to know nothing among you except Jesus Christ, and Him crucified" (1 Cor 2:2 NASB). A young student accepted the Lord. I was thrilled. I met with the committee, who were mighty good folks and mostly related to OSU. We stayed in contact. Veta delivered Mark David, our third child, on March 27, 1963. Plans fell into place, and we moved to Stillwater in May. For now, God was telling us that the pastorate was where we belonged.

Leaving McKinney was difficult. We had such a good youth group and a great group of young adults as well. We still stay in touch with a few of them each Christmas. The church had been so good to us for the four years that we were there. Bailey Stone treated us well. I enjoyed my roles there; however, this ministry was not what I felt the Lord wanted me to do long-term. We rolled out of town in a Chevrolet station wagon—Donny and Debbie playing in the back with the seat down and Veta holding David in her arms—to begin another chapter in ministry.

Stillwater is in north central Oklahoma. I-35 runs north from Texas through Oklahoma and beyond, and Stillwater is about fifteen miles east on US 51. Oklahoma State had sixteen thousand students in 1963, and the town of Stillwater had a population of about thirteen thousand at the time. Consequently, when school began in the fall, the town more than doubled in size. University Heights had grown out of First Baptist, Stillwater in 1954. A group desiring to have a better ministry to students bought a house (the old Baptist Student Union building) one block from campus. When we came on the scene, the church was struggling in many ways. For instance, they had to take collections each month for three Sundays in a row before they were able to pay the previous month's bills. In the past ten years the church had purchased three houses for education space. A meetinghouse, which would seat four hundred, stood on the back lots of two of those houses. A two-story house, which had been a fraternity house, served as Sunday School space for the college students. This house was behind the meetinghouse on an adjacent street. With the exception of the meetinghouse, the facilities left a lot to be desired. The support staff included three part-time folks—secretary, music director, and caretaker. The spirit of the church, fortunately, was top-notch. The members were simply looking for someone to love and serve them.

Finding a place to live in Stillwater was a hurdle. The University faculty and students had gobbled up all available facilities. For the first three months we lived in an apartment. And then a door opened. The oldest house in Payne County was the Duck house, a frame house built in 1889 by a Sooner who made the run from the Kansas border.[1] When he passed from the scene, his daughter turned it into a rental property. Word came to the church of its availability, and this house became our domicile for the next two years. I had a good time playing in the big side yard with our kids and the neighborhood kids, too. Donny was five and Debbie was two at the time. One day several kids came up to our side door and said, "Mrs. Sherman, will you let Dr. Sherman come out and play with us?" This situation reminded us of the words of Art Linkletter, "Kids say the darndest things."

We had very few middle-aged or senior adults; however, we had a fine group of young adults. Many of these were graduate students working on advanced degrees. The makeup of our congregation gave us plenty of young boys and girls, so we began planning for Vacation Bible School. Our VBS ran Monday through Friday from 9:00 a.m. until noon. It was a time of great

---

[1] "Sooner" is the name given to settlers who entered the Indian Territory, now Oklahoma, prior to the official start of the Land Rush of 1889.

fun for our workers as well as for the boys and girls, and it provided an opportunity for us to become better acquainted with our church members.

Later that summer we had a men's retreat. I shared with the fellows that we needed to spruce up our facilities to attract new members. All the houses needed painting, as did the meetinghouse. I encouraged each man to buy a gallon of Sherwin-Williams paint and show up for six Saturdays to help give the place a facelift. They bought in, and the next Saturday we tackled the job like a bunch of Seabees. It was a hoot! We worked, we laughed, we became better acquainted, and we finished the job! Our facilities benefited, and we became a band of brothers. Many of the rooms were not air-conditioned—and boy, does it get hot in Oklahoma in the summertime. So we took up a special offering and put window air-conditioning units in the children's Sunday School rooms and in the college assembly room. When OSU cranked up that fall, the students came back to a church with a new look. Church folk are at their best when they worship and work together. The summer had been a profitable one.

Come fall 1963, our church hit the ground running. During the first two Sundays of September, over one hundred college students joined the church. There was a new spirit of enthusiasm and a great atmosphere in which to preach. Students keep you on your toes. You must be on target with your information and illustrations, and they are responsive to any humor appropriately shared. I looked forward to the Sunday sermons. Before the Sunday night ministries, our church provided a light supper for students called Dine-a-mite. This time gave me a chance to mix and mingle and really get to know our students. On Wednesday nights we had Bible study. I always prepared a page covering the theme or chapter that I wanted to address to make the study worth the students' time. I also wanted them to know that I was prepared, for some of the pastors I had grown up with did not do their homework for Wednesday nights. I liked to serve up the great ideas of a passage and then have those in attendance volley with me, as in a tennis game—mentally and spiritually—so we could learn together.

One of the pluses we had going for us was OSU's Baptist Student Union, which had an active ministry for Baptists and other Christians on campus. The BSU center was ideally located on the main street at the front of campus. Shortly after I came to UHBC, the state convention named John Scales the BSU director. We became great friends and were mutually supportive of each other's ministries. John ran a great ship. He related to the students and they to him. The BSU held a vesper service each Monday night with over one hundred students in attendance. I went as much as I was able to. From time to time John had the pastor from one of the four Baptist churches in Stillwater—First, University Heights, North, and South—speak to the BSU. Accepting an invitation one week, I put on my bib overalls. When I walked in, everyone was a bit surprised. Standing to give the devotional, I announced my message—"Christianity in Overalls." The thrust of the message was for us to live the faith daily as anyone can fake it on Sunday. Dr. Maston aptly said, "Christianity is not how high you jump on Sunday, but how straight you walk every day of the week." For years after that devotional, students came up to me and said, "Dr. Sherman, the one devotional that I fondly remember is when you walked into the BSU in those crazy overalls."

Our first year in Stillwater was marked by a significant event—Donny started the first grade. Westwood Elementary School was one block from our house. Veta registered him, and the big day came. We asked him if he wanted us to go with him on his first day, but he said, "No." So we all went into the yard to give him a send-off. Veta held David in her arms, and I held Debbie's hand. We told Donny to be careful, and he walked down the sidewalk like he owned the town. We stood and watched with no one saying a word. When he came to the edge of the school playground, he turned around and waved. We waved back. Then he walked into the school. We turned to each other and smiled, with tears in our eyes, and walked back into the house.

Our first year at UHBC seemed to fly by. The year was a good and meaningful one. We eventually discovered, however, that there was a long-standing issue in the church. A dean and his wife were highly involved in the college Sunday School, and he had long used his position of authority to manipulate and control church decision-making. Members of the congregation remained silent in church business meetings knowing that to speak out and cross the dean had consequential fallout on campus. Church members privately shared their feelings with me in confidence. I had to address the situation. Times like this are when a pastor earns his money. I have always felt that you need to be honest and open in dealing with issues in a church family. However, I felt that a conversation such as this was more appropriately dealt with in a private setting. I met with the dean and his wife and tried in a kind and honest way to explain to them the lay of the land. I had never been in a situation like this, and I hoped for understanding and an adjustment on their parts. Unfortunately, they were less than agreeable, to put it mildly. The dialogue lasted for fifteen to twenty minutes and was not redemptive. I tried to graciously share with them that in a Baptist church everyone has a say, and we all work for the good of the whole. I left pretty much knowing that I would not be on their Christmas card list at the end of the year. However, when the rest of the congregation learned of my efforts, they were deeply appreciative and knew that in the future we would conduct our church business evenhandedly, with all persons having an equal vote and voice. We moved on.

After renting the Duck house for over a year, I approached our deacons with a plan. The church was giving us $75 a month for a housing allowance. I shared with the men that we would gladly give that back to the church as a monthly payment if the congregation built a parsonage. If the church raised a down payment and got a loan, the church could use the $75 each month to pay off the loan. The church would benefit by getting a parsonage, and we would have a house. They bought in. Now the joy of living in a town like Stillwater came into play. A. Frank Martin, a trustee at our church, went to the bank and secured a $25,000

Family picture, Christmas of 1966, in Stillwater, Oklahoma.

loan without a down payment. He assured the bank that the church would meet their obligation, or he would underwrite the loan himself. He walked across the street to the Shelton Lumber Company. Jack Shelton, the owner, had been friends with Frank for years. Frank talked him into building the house. When Frank told the church what he had done, the membership was pleased. We promised the church that Veta and I would bird-dog the construction, and if any construction charges exceeded the $25,000, we would pay for them ourselves. For the next four months we watched the building of the parsonage, and the church budget was not altered one penny. When we moved in, everybody involved was happy.

On our twelfth wedding anniversary we were sitting at the supper table when I looked at my watch and said, "Veta, do you remember what we were doing twelve years ago at this time?" She said, "Yes, I was getting ready to walk down the aisle at our wedding." I turned to Debbie, who was four, and said, "Debbie, would you like to have come to Mother and Daddy's wedding?" She giggled and said, "Oh, yes!" Donny, the wiser, older brother, lifted his chin and said pontifically, "Debbie, don't you know that very few children get to go to their mother and daddy's wedding?" Veta and I burst out laughing, and we still laugh every time we think of this story.

One of the highlights of the summer at UHBC was taking a group of college students to Glorieta for student week. While we did not go our very first summer in 1963, we went every other summer while we were in Stillwater. In 1964 Veta and I enjoyed the conference, the students, and the leadership. In 1965 I led several groups. In 1966 the Sunday School Board invited me to preach the Sunday evening service to about 1,800 students and leaders—a challenging assignment. I preached a sermon entitled "The Compulsion of the Cross." The cross compels us "to believe and believe strongly; to act and act greatly; and to love and love supremely." Glorieta was an inspiring time for me. Many of the Baptist student directors from various colleges and universities had been Baylor and Southwestern friends. That week an unusual event occurred.

Eighteen months earlier in winter 1965, I received a phone call at 10:30 p.m. The temperature was in the 20s, sleet was falling, and the wind was blowing in at about fifteen miles per hour from the northwest. The voice on the other end of the line was a freshman girl. Through sobs she asked, "Dr. Sherman, will you come over to Murray Hall and talk with me? I have a big problem." I responded, "In light of the weather could we visit in the morning? I'll be happy to talk with you." The next voice was from the housemother, who said, "Pastor, although it is past hours, I will let you in. This young lady needs help." I replied, "I'm on my way." I got up, dressed, and slid down to the campus. The weather was bitter. Ice covered the steps. The housemother met me and led me to the parlor where a distraught young lady was waiting. She was a freshman who had joined our church earlier in the fall. She had just found out that she was pregnant. An older boy from her hometown was involved. We talked, and I tried to console her. I shared that she could find forgiveness and begin anew thanks to the grace of God. She said, "I've asked the Lord to forgive me." However, she had one more request. Her parents were coming to Homecoming in another week. She asked, "Will you let them come to your office at church where I can tell them? I'm afraid that my father will beat me when he hears. He won't do that in your office." That was a new twist. I assured her that I would try to help, and yes, she could bring her parents to my office on Saturday morning.

I shared the story with Veta the next morning at breakfast. We both began to pray that things would stay between the fences. Saturday came, and I went to my office. I was a bit apprehensive to say the least. My office was down a long hall—the last room on the right. Before long I heard footsteps coming down the hall. In walked the young girl and her parents. She said, "Dr. Sherman, I want you to meet my parents. They're from western Oklahoma." I invited them in, and everyone sat down. The father was a rancher and strongly built. When we shook hands, I felt like I was shaking hands with a vise. The mother was reserved. We sat awkwardly. The father said, "Well, Reverend, it's been nice meeting you; but we'd better move on. We don't want to miss the parade." He stood up and turned to the door. I said, "Mr. _____, thank you for coming; however, your daughter has something to tell you." He froze, turned to her, and said, "Now just what have you been into?" She burst into tears and said, "Now, Daddy. Now, Daddy. Now, Daddy!" The situation was going south very quickly. He raised his voice and said,

"What have you done? Are you pregnant?" She nodded. He said, "Tell me who he is. I'm going after him right now. He'll be sorry when I finish with him. Tell me. Tell me!" I stood and said, "Mr. _____, we are not in a good situation. Let's don't make it worse." He stared at me, took a deep breath, and sat down. He then said, "If you can have him in this room in the next hour, we'll work something out. If he's not here, I'm going after him."

Things calmed down a bit. She told her parents who he was. He was an upperclassman from her hometown whom she had dated in high school. The families knew each other. I asked for his phone number, and she gave it to me. They left to get a bite of breakfast, planning to return within the hour. I dialed the number and had one of the most bizarre telephone conversations of my life. He answered the phone, and I told him who I was. He responded, "So-o-o-o-o?" I told him he needed to come to my office within the hour. He said, "Can't come, Preach, I'm going to the parade." I said, "Buddy, the _____ family just left my office. Their daughter told her parents she was pregnant. Her dad said he was coming after you if you were not here in an hour. You get the message?" After a long pause the voice hesitantly said, "I'll be there."

I must say that the hour passed slowly. I called Veta and told her what had taken place. She expressed concern for my safety. I told her that I hoped we could keep things within boundaries. I asked the Lord for big-time help. Then the parents and daughter returned. The atmosphere was somber. We made small talk. I shared that although the situation was dire, we needed to do our best to come to some arrangement that would be in the best interest of all parties involved. About that time we heard rapid footsteps coming down the long hall. A six-foot-tall young man came through the door. He was scared and hyperventilating. The father stood up and called his name. The young man started repeating, "Now, _____. Now, _____! Hold on. Hold on!" I stood up and asked everyone to please sit down. They did, and for about forty-five minutes a heated dialogue ensued. Eventually everyone agreed to the following arrangement: the girl would drop out of school at midterm and go to Denver, Colorado, where her brother and his family lived. She would deliver the child and place it for adoption. The boy would pay for all expenses. The parents insisted that he have no additional contact or communication with their daughter in the future. Finally, the encounter drew to a close, and I ended the meeting with a prayer.

I drove home about noon, emotionally shot. For the next three months the young man came to my office and handed me a check that I forwarded to Colorado. After that I never saw him again. The whole experience had been bruising for everyone.

This story has a redemptive ending, and it happened a year and a half later while I was preaching at Glorieta. I had just finished my sermon at Glorieta, and we were going to get Debbie in the nursery. As we were standing in the courtyard a young lady came up to me and said, "Dr. Sherman, do you remember me?" She was the same young lady who sat pregnant in my office that day. I was amazed. I called her by name and gave her a big hug. I was so glad to see her. She had a big smile on her face and said, "Dr. Sherman, God is so good." I replied, "Tell me your story; why are you here?" She shared that she had found God's forgiveness. After releasing the baby girl for adoption, she had enrolled at Texas Tech University in Lubbock. She was now engaged to a ministerial student who planned to enroll at Golden Gate Seminary in California in the fall. After their wedding in August, they would move to California. Again, she said, "God is so good!" Meeting her and hearing her testimony was the best thing that happened to me that entire week, confirming what I already knew from Romans—where sin did abound, grace did superabound.

One of the tragedies that occurred during our time in Stillwater was the death of three of our finest students—Steve Green, Barbara Faulkner, and David Hodges—in a car wreck on Highway 51. They were active in the BSU and highly involved in our student group at church. We knew each of them well. Their deaths really hit the campus, the BSU, and our church folks hard. I conducted the memorial services for Steve and David. Steve lived in an apartment in our Sunday School building. He unlocked the church buildings every Sunday, turned on the lights, and monitored the building temperature. He loved David, our youngest, and would hoist him up in his arms each Sunday night, carrying him around to turn off the lights. Steve was engaged to one of our finest, Sybil Zumbro, and they planned to be married come summer. I was to officiate their wedding. Sybil asked if I would go with her to return her engagement ring to the jeweler and her announcements to the printer. The situation was heartbreaking. When you pastor a college church, some of the students come to be family. We still send Christmas cards and visit by phone with them 'til this day, over a half century later. Such are the joys and sorrows of serving a church.

As the years rolled by the church experienced good growth. In 1965 we added an early worship service, which 150 to 200 would attend. The 11:00 a.m. service saw about four hundred in attendance, 80 percent of whom were students. In 1966, when the SBC began the Southern Baptists' Missionary Journeyman program for young adults, I invited Louis Cobbs from the Foreign Mission Board to challenge our students to climb on board. A journeyman volunteered to spend two years of his or her life on the mission field assisting the vocational missionaries. Right out of the box, Phil Caskey volunteered to sign up. He spent two years in the Philippines in Dagupan City. I read his letters to our congregation. Phil inspired Janie Tyler to go to Indonesia. Incidentally, she found an extra perk when she married Rob Sellers, who was also a journeyman. David Moncrief served as a summer missionary. When these students returned and told their stories, everyone—young and old—was inspired.

One Saturday afternoon in August 1967, Donny and I were in the front yard mowing the lawn when a car pulled up. The driver was Jim Harris, the high school football coach and a good friend. He played football for Oklahoma A&M about the same time that I played for Baylor. I said, "Jim, glad to see you. Are you ready to begin fall workouts?" He replied, "Preacher, that's why I'm here. I hired a coach from Bartlesville who was supposed to move this summer. He called this morning, and he's not coming. Would you come out and help me coach the Pioneers this fall? Monday morning, I'm gonna have eighty-five players on my hands, and I need some help." I told Jim that I appreciated the gesture, but I had never coached before. He said, "Listen, Bill, you've played the game. I can go down to Skeen's Cafeteria and make an appeal, and I'll have a bunch of guys who don't know what they're doing." I took the plan to the deacons on Sunday afternoon, and I was on the high school workout field Monday afternoon.

Each weekday I would leave the church at 3:00 p.m., go out to the high school, and ask Jim, "Who do you want me work with today, and what is the scheme?" He would lay out the plan, and I would do what he asked. I loved my job; I truly believe I could have been a coach as a vocation. We only had one starter from the previous year; however, we had a group of talented juniors who were tough and coachable. Stillwater was a 2A school with over five hundred students. Our first game was against Broken Arrow High School just outside of Tulsa. We were the underdogs. Guess what? We beat them. The next game was against Putnam City, a 3A school. We lost a close one to a team that ended up 3A champions that year. The third game was in Norman, at University of Oklahoma's stadium, to another 3A school. We lost by seven. We then won seven straight games, putting us into the state playoffs. I invited the team to church so we could recognize them as district champions. They filled four rows in the center section. I told the congregation that in three weeks they would be back as state champions.

A state championship would take two more wins. Our first opponent was Altus. The game was a knock-down-drag-out for four quarters, and Stillwater was the last team standing. We had one more hurdle to the championship—Okmulgee.

The game was a toss-up. We led in the fourth quarter by four points. Okmulgee made a frenetic drive in the last two minutes. They had the ball on our twelve-yard line with twenty seconds to go. Their quarterback looked into the end zone and wheeled a dart into the left flat. But our cornerback stepped in front of the receiver, intercepted the pass, and ran ninety yards for a touchdown as time ran out! What a way to win a championship. Two mornings later the Stillwater Pioneer football team filled three rows of the center section at University Heights Baptist Church. I proudly introduced them as the 1967 State Champions of Division 2A in the state of Oklahoma. The congregation gave them a two-minute standing ovation. What a great fall we had! I was there to be a coach, but I also hoped to be a genuine Christian witness. Coach Harris and I spent about an hour taping the ankles of the team members before all the games. Everyone sat around waiting his turn. We all participated in the various conversations, sharing jokes from time to time. One night as I was taping the ankles of our tight end, he said, "Coach Sherman, you know more funny jokes than anybody I know, and the most amazing thing is that all of them are clean." Hopefully, in an indirect way, the players got the message.

One Sunday night after we came home from church, I went into Debbie's room to tell her good night. She was sitting up in bed, pensive. Though the light in the hall was on, the room was dark. I said, "Honey, are you alright?" She paused and said, "Daddy, I believe Jesus is calling me to become a Christian." She then burst into tears. I hugged her and asked if she wanted to talk further about how she was feeling. She shook her head sideways. I told her when she did, I would be glad to talk to her. A few days later she came and said she was ready to talk. She prayed and invited Jesus into her heart. Her conversion was a precious and sacred moment. The next Sunday she made her confession known before the church. I had the joy of baptizing her. The year was 1967.

I was the morning preacher at Glorieta for student week during summer 1967 where I did a sermon series on Jesus' encounters. The first sermon was entitled "Jesus and the Hippie" on Jesus' encounter with the woman at the well. The second was "Jesus and Mr. Gotrocks" on Jesus and the rich young ruler. The third was "Jesus and Mr. Brain" on Jesus and Nicodemus. The fourth was "Jesus and Mr. Nobody" on Jesus and blind Bartimaeus. And the last message was "Jesus and Joe College" on Jesus and Nicodemus. The sermons were well-received. What I did not realize was that Carlton Carter, who worked in the Training

Union department of the Sunday School Board and who was a member of Woodmont Baptist Church in Nashville, Tennessee, was recording them. Dr. Allen West, Woodmont's pastor of twenty-five years, had just moved to Louisville, Kentucky, to be the superintendent of missions for the Long Run Baptist Association. Consequently, Carlton gave the tapes to the pulpit search committee, writing me a nice letter in the process sharing what he had done. Veta and I read the letter, having no idea what might come from his actions.

A few months later, on a Wednesday night at 10:35 p.m., the phone rang. The voice at the other end of the line said, "Are you Dr. Bill Sherman?" I did not recognize the voice—a deep bass with a Southern drawl. I replied, "What's left of him." He said, "This is Dr. Maurice Bull, and I am the chairman of the pulpit search committee at the Woodmont Baptist Church in Nashville, Tennessee. This call in no way obligates the Woodmont Baptist Church to you or you to the Woodmont Baptist Church." That surprised me. I responded kindly, "Dr. Bull, we are perfectly happy where we are, and you have the problem." He chuckled and said, "Would you be willing to talk with us about the possibility of becoming our pastor?" I replied, "Veta and I are open to any door that the Lord might lead us through. We would not encourage you or discourage you from talking with us. We want to be open to the Lord's leadership." Such was the opening conversation with the Woodmont pulpit committee, a conversation that would lead to our move to Nashville.

7
WOODMONT BAPTIST, NASHVILLE, TENNESSEE

1968–1969

After a great deal of soul-searching, Veta and I felt it important to be open to the Woodmont inquiry. We loved Stillwater, and we enjoyed our ministry to the students; however, we continually sought to be where God wanted us to be. We shared these thoughts with the Woodmont search committee, which led to three members of the committee flying to Stillwater. We spent Saturday and Sunday together, and they heard me preach. Our entire family then flew to Nashville for a three-day visit. The pieces came together, and Woodmont called us in November 1967.

Leaving University Heights was a hard task. For almost five years we had plowed our energy into that college church. The members had become family, and the students had become our sons and daughters. We had learned more about designing ministries to meet people where they are in life. While in Stillwater, I finished my dissertation, the last requirement of my Doctorate in Theology degree.

When we drove out of town, Veta and I truly felt like Paul when he wrote to the Philippians, "I thank my God upon every remembrance of you" (Phil 1:3 KJV). Yet, we had a peace and wondered what the future held in Nashville as we headed the station wagon east on I-40 into the sunrise.

We arrived in Nashville on Friday, December 29, 1967 and unloaded the moving van all the next day. The parsonage was a two-story Georgian house with a full basement. To speed things up I carried boxes in for most of the day—ten steps up to the back door and twelve steps up to the second floor. By nightfall my body was suing my legs for non-support. A number of church members stopped by to welcome us throughout the day. We turned in tired, yet with great anticipation for the next day—Sunday. What a huge surprise we would have!

I awoke about 5:45 a.m. As I lay in bed, I noticed how bright everything was outdoors. I arose and went to the window to see snow coming down to beat the band. It covered everything, including about an inch on the clothesline. The scene was straight from a picture on a Christmas card. I exclaimed, "Good honk," which awakened Veta. She asked what was going on. When I told her to come and look, she cried, "My heavens, what will we do about church?" The snow was nine inches deep. About this time the phone rang. Red Harden, chairman of the deacons, asked in his distinct Southern drawl, "Pastah, have you looked out the window?" I replied, "Yes, Red." He inquired, "What do you think we ought to do about worship?" I answered, "Red, we have been here for two days. You all know better as to what we should do, I suspect." He said, "Well, I would surely hate for us to call off services on your first Sunday. However, in the past when there has been ice and snow, we have had church members' cars slide into other members' cars in the parking lot, and it has strained the fellowship!" So we called off services on our first Sunday. I told Veta that we would simply unpack boxes and watch a worship service on the television. Well, guess what? There was not a single worship service of any persuasion on television. I told Veta that this should be corrected in a city like Nashville. We would later revisit that idea.

In Baptist life at that time, Nashville was the hub of many ministries. The executive offices of the Southern Baptist denomination were located there as well as the Baptist Sunday School Board. Several hundred folks from these two entities were members of Baptist churches throughout the city. Woodmont was one of these churches. In those years there was an overall harmony in the denomination, making it a good time to be a Baptist.

Woodmont came into being in August 1941. The church was in the southwest part of Nashville in a country area known as Green Hills. Roy Greene was the owner of Green Hills Market. While checking his patrons out, he asked if any would be interested in starting a church. The interest was there, and formal meetings began to discuss the nuts and bolts. After several weeks of meetings, the constitution service was set for Hillsboro High School. The small group committed to forming a congregation and began meeting on Sundays at the school. Their numbers multiplied, and in December they called Dr. Allen West as pastor. He had just finished his doctorate program at Southern Baptist Seminary in Louisville, Kentucky. He and his beloved wife, Kitty, served the congregation for twenty-five years. Allen was a great people person, a capable preacher, and a servant pastor. He gave good leadership to the folk at Woodmont for a quarter of a century. He and Kitty had a son, George, and a daughter, Janet. They and their families were faithful church members through the years as well. Allen was my friend, and we enjoyed a great relationship.

World War II slowed the congregation's ability to construct facilities. However, in 1944 they built a chapel, followed in 1948 by an education building, and in 1956 by a large meetinghouse that could seat 1,400 people. These were the facilities that were in place when we came on the scene. Don Mauldin was the minister of education, and Clay Killion was the minister of music. Support staff included Martha Nelson, Joanne James, and Martha Putnam. We all hit the trail together to continue the work that Allen West had begun.

The Christian Life Commission had designated the second Sunday in February as Race Relations Sunday on the denominational calendar. I chose to preach a sermon entitled "Just Call Him Brother." I was aware that I was now a resident of the Old South. I was also aware of the fact that the silence of many white Christians had reinforced the customs that had kept African Americans as second-class citizens. Civil rights was a hot topic. Abuses based on race were happening all over the South. I determined to be part of the solution instead of part of the problem. In my sermon introduction I asked how many remembered a song we had learned in our early Sunday School years—"Jesus Loves the Little Children." Everybody nodded. I asked the congregation to sing the song, ". . . red and yellow, black and white, They are precious in His sight, Jesus loves the little children of the world." I went on to say that if we treat each person as Jesus treated him or her, our race situation would be solved. The sermon was well-received . . . by most members of the congregation.

On Tuesday afternoon two charter members of the church appeared unannounced at my office. One had been on the pastor search committee. We made small talk for a few minutes. Then one said, "Preacher, if you have any more sermons in your file like the one last Sunday, leave them in the file." I was not totally surprised. I answered, "My preaching will be as Martin Luther said at the Diet of Worms, '. . . my conscience is captive to the Word of God. . . . Here I stand, I can do no other.'" I went on to ask if anything I said in the sermon was unbiblical. They said, "No." Thankfully, the continued exchange between us was civil. One countered, "Preacher, you need to preach the Gospel and not get off on these tangents." I responded, "This is the gospel. The gospel is for the whole person. Do you remember Christ's parable of the Good Samaritan? Christ is interested in how we treat one another as well as our relationship to God in conversion." The conversation went on for about forty-five minutes. Our visit was not heated and ended amiably. One said, "Well, we are not going to agree, but at least we know where we stand." We shook hands, and they left.

In spring 1968 our youth choir presented the youth musical *Good News*, which the congregation enjoyed. The young people were upbeat and enjoyed the songs from A to Z. This was during the days in which hippies were on the scene in a big way. In the middle of the musical, the script had a group of young people coming down each of the aisles singing, "I'm a rebel. Yes, I am. I'm a rebel. That's me, man. It doesn't matter what you say, for I'll be headed in the other way!" The "rebels" were some of our youth choir members disguised with hippie gear and makeup. I was sitting on the second row with three of our senior adults seated right behind me. They leaned forward and exclaimed, "Dr. Sherman, call the ushers. We need to show these hippies the door." I tried to keep a straight face as I replied, "They're part of the musical." They looked surprised and said, "Oh!"

In summer 1968 we took a survey of the Brentwood community, an outlying area six miles south of Nashville, where Woodmont had bought twelve acres a year or so before as a possible site for a new church. Woodmont excelled in this kind of expansion. In the previous twenty years Woodmont had started missions in Brook Hollow, Forest Hills, Crievewood, and Glenwood. Deacons gathered on this Sunday afternoon, and we walked from house to house sharing our plan. At the end of six weeks, we sent a circular to all those who had shown an interest. On a Sunday afternoon eighteen excited people gathered in the chapel of the Baptist Children's Home in response to the circular. Each Sunday afternoon thereafter we held a service led by preachers from our congregation. A year later the mission organized into a church with over three hundred members. They called Bill Wilson Sr. as their pastor the following year.

In 1969 we revisited the idea of a television ministry. Channel 17 was a new station in Nashville, a UHF station. I discussed the idea with the deacons, and they bought in. Next, we went to the finance committee. A television ministry would cost $25,000 a year. To underwrite the ministry, we decided to take this amount from the mission's section of the budget. We explained in full to the church membership that we believed in the importance of the mission and that we would fully restore the money the following year. Everyone seemed amenable. I almost thought the discussion at this point was overkill. Just as we were to vote on the matter, a long-standing member who worked at the Sunday School Board stood up. He said, "Dr. Sherman, Dr. Sherman. Stand up and look me in the eye; I have something to say to you." I stood up. He said, "You have led this church away from the Cooperative Program. God will not bless this church if we vote to do this. I pray its rejection. May God have mercy on us." I was shocked that this man had personalized the issue. I countered, "Dr. ___,

Dr. ____. Stand up and look me in the eye. You have the right to vote your conscience on this matter. However, you do not have the right to personalize the issue. I ask all members to vote their conscience. If a member feels an evangelical outreach to the city for Christ is worthy, so be it. I assure you that we will restore the monies to the mission's section as promised." The members were stunned. Our deacon moderator quietly said, "I believe we have discussed this matter long enough. All in favor, and all not in favor." The motion overwhelmingly passed. Such is how our television ministry began. We replaced the mission's money in 1970.

The television ministry began in 1969 with between eight thousand and ten thousand viewers tuning in each Sunday. I began by welcoming the television congregation to the service, and I said a further word to them during the offering. I wanted the service to be personal to them. I further shared that this was a Christian worship service, not just a Baptist one. I also encouraged them to send their offerings to their own churches. This worship service was to declare that forgiveness is through Christ, and through Him we can have a right relationship with God. Having established the playing field, we moved on with the worship service. As time went by, more and more folk began to join our television congregation.

A tragic accident occurred in 1969. Jim Killion, the son of our minister of music and his wife, was involved in a deadly accident on Harding Road when a drunk college student ran a light and crashed into the rear of his car. Paramedics rushed him to Baptist Hospital where he was comatose and placed on a ventilator. Within an hour forty to fifty Woodmont folks were there. We prayed and hoped through the night (Saturday). The next morning our church was in shock. I could hardly get through my sermon without crying. Our folks came in such numbers to the hospital that the administrator asked me to tell them to go home. Five days later, Jim died. A cloud hung over our congregation for weeks. People became closer, and everyone lifted each other up. The members "[bore] one another's burdens, and so fulfill[ed] the law of Christ" (Gal 6:2 ESV).

On a Wednesday afternoon in early fall 1969, I received a telephone call from Kathleen Horrell. She asked if she and her husband, Henry, might drop by the parsonage after prayer meeting. I said we would be delighted to receive them. The Horrells were some of the finest members in the congregation. He was a deacon of long standing. She taught one of the best ladies' Sunday School classes in the church. When I hung up the phone I said to Veta with a chuckle, "I wonder what they want to talk about. I can't believe they are having marital problems." We gathered in the living room later that evening. Kathleen said, "Pastor, what are you doing the last two weeks of October? Henry and I would like to make an investment in your ministry. We would like to take you and Veta to Paris, Cairo, Lebanon, and all over Israel, and Rome. Would you like to go?" Veta and I were blown away. I could not quite believe my ears. She said again, "Would you like to go?" I said, "Kathleen, is there a cow in Texas? Why, yes, we would be thrilled to go!" Come fall we flew to each of those historic places. I could not believe our blessings.

Finally, the time for our trip arrived. We flew all night and did not sleep much. We had a four-hour layover in Paris, so rather than cool our heels in the airport, we rented a cab. We visited Notre Dame Cathedral where a mass was in progress. We visited Napoleon's Tomb and saw his marble sarcophagus. We drove by the remains of the Bastille, which the citizens charged in 1789 to trigger the French Revolution. We drove by the Louvre and the Arc de Triomphe and down the Champs-Élysées to the foot of the Eiffel Tower. That was one of the best cab rides I have ever taken. We then flew to Cairo where we arrived after dark.

The next day we took in the Egyptian Museum where we saw the mummy of King Tut and other pharaohs. We took a camel ride around the Great Pyramid of Khufu, one of the Seven Wonders of the Ancient World, and had our pictures taken in front of the Sphinx. The next morning, we flew to Lebanon where we visited Byblos and Baalbek, two of the oldest cities on the eastern shores of the Mediterranean. The following day we visited the amazing ruins of Tyre and Sidon. We then flew to Tel Aviv and on

First trip to Egypt, October of 1969—Bill and Veta are on far right, back row.

to the sites of Jerusalem, Bethlehem, and Golgotha. We drove by bus to Galilee. One of the prettiest areas we saw was around the Sea of Galilee. I read the Sermon on the Mount to our group at the Horns of Hattin, the likeliest site of the sermon.

Having finished our time in the Levant, we flew to Rome. We could have spent a month in the Vatican Museum and not have seen it all. The Coliseum was overwhelming. In the Forum we saw the grave of Julius Caesar. Our last visit was to the Roman Basilica in Vatican Square and the Sistine Chapel. We flew home with a boatload of memories but anxious to see our kids again.

Donny was ten years old when we made the move to Nashville. He was in the fifth grade at Woodmont Elementary. Debbie was in the second grade at Woodmont Elementary. She made friends easily and loved her teacher. David was four and a great help to Veta at home. He entered the Woodmont Baptist kindergarten when he was five. Fortunately, there were other children in our neighborhood. Dr. Andy and Sue Spickard, who had a son and daughter about the ages of Donny and Debbie, lived next door. Dr. Jim and Carolyn Brakefield, who had a son and daughter about the same ages as our kids as well, lived across the street. Our backyard became the football and wiffle ball field. I loved to play with the kids. One afternoon a funny thing happened. David and Anderson were doing something I had asked them not to do. I opened the door and stepped onto the porch and said, "Kids, if you do that again I'm going to bust your can!" I turned to go back in the house, and Anderson, with a high soprano voice, said, "Dr Sherman, what is a can?" I got so tickled I could hardly talk for laughing. David said, "Anderson, it's your behind." Anderson exclaimed, "Oh!" Growing up on Sterling Road was fun.

8
WOODMONT AND RACE RELATIONS

1970–1972

I felt good about our church as we began 1970. Thankfully, we were growing. Over 130 folks had united with us either by letter or by baptism in 1969. The television ministry was also expanding. At that time, Clay Killion, our minister of music, felt led to accept a call from a fine church in Tulsa, Oklahoma. He and his wife, Bobadell, hoped that a change of venue might give them some healing from losing their son Jim. Ray Connor became the interim director of music and did a splendid job. A few months later, we called Charles Downey as minister of music. Woodmont's mission outreach church at Brentwood now had over 350 each Sunday. Our church had given them the twelve acres in downtown Brentwood.

The issue of busing to achieve school integration was a contentious topic in Nashville. Our mayoral election coincided with the Supreme Court's debate in *Swann v. Charlotte-Mecklenburg Board of Education*. A Baptist deacon at a neighbor church was running for mayor. He claimed, "If you elect me as mayor, no child will be bused in Nashville." This claim was bogus as the busing issue was a national issue dictated by federal law, not a local issue. I felt led to preach about the topic since God calls Christians to be law-abiding citizens. In the sermon, I affirmed that first, believers are to obey the laws of the land as Paul wrote in Romans 13. Second, I stressed that Christians should be bridge builders in race relations. Third, I emphasized that as Christians we should reach out to all races. Those in Nashville who felt that such a message was long overdue applauded the effort.

About that time a leadership group of the Fifteenth Avenue Baptist Church invited me to speak. This congregation in north Nashville was one of the largest African American churches in the city. When the time came for this meeting, I waited for my turn to speak. As I sat there, I introduced myself to the gentleman beside me—Enoch Jones, the pastor of the church. During the break I had a chance to run an idea by him. I said, "Enoch, our town needs the witness of a white and Black church to show how Christians should relate to each other. How would it be if our two churches led the way?" He replied, "That sounds good, Bill, but how are we going to do it?" I suggested we have a joint worship service and said, "You preach at our church on Sunday morning with your choir singing the special music. The service will be on television for the whole town to see. On Sunday night I will preach in your pulpit with our choir providing the special music." He replied, "Bill, that sounds good, but can we pull this off?" I told him I did not know for sure, but I felt like we should try. We agreed to take up the idea at a later time.

In January 1971 I felt led to bring the idea of the joint service to our deacons. I discussed the idea first with our deacon chairman, Herschel Bryant, as I did not want him to be blindsided. He said, "Preacher, you know this will have some pushback; yet it is something that our church should do." I wrote a letter to our deacons sharing the basic tenets of the joint service and explaining why I felt the service would be redemptive for our church and city. Needless to say, the topic helped with attendance—we had thirty-two deacons present. I was hopeful that everyone would behave themselves. Actually, the meeting became the most inspirational deacons' meeting of my sixty-six-year ministry.

We sat in a wide semicircle and discussed routine preliminary issues first. Everybody was delighted that for the first time since 1947, we had not only made our budget but exceeded it by $416. As one deacon said, "This is something to write home about!" The laughter was sincere but apprehensive. Our chairman then said, "Fellas, our pastor has an idea to share with us which he feels could be redemptive for our church and city." I stood up and explained what I had in mind, though the men were basically in the know from my letter. I then shared why I felt the service would be a good witness to our city.

Race relations were tense throughout the nation and the South. In 1961 the Freedom Riders bus was burned in Anniston, Alabama. In 1963 Medgar Evers was shot in Jackson, Mississippi. Around six hundred marchers were beaten and attacked by dogs on the bridge in Selma, Alabama, in 1965. Martin Luther King was assassinated in 1968. I simply said, "Somebody needs to be the light. Somebody needs to break the silence. I know a racially integrated service will be uncomfortable for some, but we are here to make a difference. I pray that Woodmont will make a difference." The men were mesmerized. No one said a word for fifteen to twenty seconds. Finally, a voice said, "I move we accept the pastor's plan." The motion received a second, and our chairman said, "Is there any discussion?"

All was quiet for another twenty seconds. Then six deacons who were sitting next to each other in the center of the semicircle began to speak one after another. The first stood and shared that this was not a good time to pursue this idea and that the preacher should stick to preaching the gospel and should not pursue other tangents. Another stood and said that we would be hypocrites if we did this, for we do not believe in racial equality ourselves. A third shared that the pastor needs to understand that he is not in Oklahoma anymore; in Tennessee we cherish our Southern culture. Each of the six men spoke, and each ended his remarks with the question—Why would we do this when we really do not believe this way? This discussion lasted about fifteen to twenty minutes. I was beginning to wonder if others would challenge these men. I took a deep breath.

What followed next was amazing. Wallace Greene, who worked at the Baptist Sunday School Board and taught the senior men's Sunday School class, stood up and said, "Gentlemen, I have sat in the pews of this church with my heart aching waiting for someone to have the courage in our pulpit to address this galling issue. Now, we have a voice with convictions. I thank God that

Dr. Sherman has broken the silence even at personal risk. He is offering a way for us to be the light in this dark world and to love one another. Further, brothers, I want you to know that we will sure enough be hypocrites if we do not accept this challenge." He sat down, and all was quiet.

Then George Eckstein, our Sunday School superintendent, stood up and said, "Brothers, I have a confession to make to you. You know that my profession has been in the sales of school supplies. I went into Black schools with my hat in one hand and my briefcase in the other so I would not have to shake hands with the Black principal. Well, I got down on my back and couldn't make my rounds for six weeks. My salary was strictly commission. We were behind with our house and car payments. Grace and I did not know how we were going to make ends meet. But one Saturday a carload of six Black principals drove to my house from West Tennessee. They sat at my dining room table and filled out orders as I told them where to look in the catalog. The commission from those orders saved us. When they left, I broke down and cried. I told Grace that I would never be prejudiced again. I am 100 percent in favor of this idea. Brothers, we will be hypocrites if we do not do this service."

Maurice Bull, a dentist and the purchasing agent for our church, was the next deacon to stand. He had been chairman of the pulpit committee when we came. He said, "Men, many of you know that I was in the Navy in World War II. I served on a Corvette, a small destroyer, in the Pacific. Japanese fighter planes strafed us, and I was hit and lost a lot of blood. We were out of transfusions. They announced on the intercom the type of blood that I needed. A Black cook walked up and volunteered to lie down on the deck and give me blood. His blood saved my life." He then took a deep breath, looked at the men, and said, "Do you want to guess which way I'm going to vote tonight?" All was quiet for at least thirty seconds. Then our chairman said, "Thank you for your input. I also wish to thank you for the way you have conducted yourselves. I believe we are ready for the vote." Twenty-five hands voted to approve the motion, six hands voted to disapprove, one deacon abstained. The meeting ended in prayer, and the brethren quietly left the room; there were no confrontations. Everyone knew the new direction of the church.

When the January business meeting took place, the chairman of the deacons shared a full explanation with the church members. The motion to approve was unanimous. We began working on the service to be held on February 21, 1971. Was there any pushback? Some. A petition quietly circulated to remove the pastor. Twenty-five people signed it. A few days later I answered the phone, and a deep bass voice drawled, "Bill, this is Enoch. Are you catching hell?" I chuckled and replied, "Well, there have been a few members take us off their Christmas card list." I then asked Enoch how his congregation was receiving the idea of a joint service. He said, "I have a few young adults who are followers of Malcolm X, and they do not want to have anything to do with white folks." We agreed to quietly make our plans and move on. The week before the joint service I received a phone call from W.A. Reed Jr., an African American religion editor for the morning paper, *The Tennessean*. We had not personally met, though I was a regular reader of his columns. He said, "Is this Bill Sherman?" I answered, "Yes." He asked, "Dr. Sherman, is it true that your church and Fifteenth Avenue are going to have a service together on February 21st?" I replied, "Yes, sir." There was a long pause at the other end of the line. He continued, "Dr. Sherman, I grew up in Nashville. I know this town and these churches, and I want to say either you are the most courageous white preacher I have ever met, or you are crazy!" I told him I did not know about the first, but he was probably right about the second. He countered and said he was glad to hear it and would be there to cover the story.

As the days drew nearer, I was angry and disgusted about one spin-off issue—nasty telephone calls. About a half dozen folks called and said some awful things. "You're a _____ lover." "Do you want your daughter to grow up and marry a _____?" "You're just craving for attention." I did not mind talking to them, but they angered me when they said these things to our kids. We received two bomb threats, which I reported to the Nashville Police Department. On the morning of the service, the police came out with a dog and checked all our buildings.

During the two years I had served at Woodmont, I had never seen the meetinghouse completely full. It could seat 1,400, including the choir loft, but we usually had around 650 to 700 in worship. That all changed on February 21. The halls were electric with excitement. Folks—Black and white—were filling the meetinghouse and exchanging greetings. All three television stations had cameras in the front foyer. Deacons from both churches sat on the front rows of all three sections. The Fifteenth Avenue choir filled the choir loft. Their minister of music, James Scandrick, was at the organ. Our minister of music, Charles Downey, had the congregation stand and sing the Doxology. The emotions were serendipity! The congregation remained standing and sang, "Holy, Holy, Holy, Lord God Almighty!" I was almost in tears. I did notice, however, that the Black and white members were sitting in clusters. At the welcome time I said, "Friends, we are believers in the same God whose Son died for us all. Now let's have a few minutes of fellowship. Let's speak and meet those of other churches. Let's also sit with each other, mix up our seating, and have salt and pepper. Let's worship the God who created us and recreated us in Jesus Christ." The strings of hesitancy seemed to loosen up, and folks began to mix and mingle. When they sat down, we were the family of God. I addressed the television audience during the offertory. I shared that this is how Christian folk get along—at the foot of the cross. Enoch Jones preached a superb sermon dotted with many "amens." That was Sunday morning.

Sunday night our folks rode two city buses over to Fifteenth Avenue Baptist Church. Others drove their cars. Our choir sang, and I preached. People packed the church house. My sermon was entitled "Our Oneness in Christ." The text was Galatians 3:28: "There is neither Jew nor Greek, there is neither slave nor free, there is neither male nor female; for you are all one in Christ Jesus" (RSV). Culture may drive races apart, but Christ brings races together. We ended the service singing, "Lord, I Want to Be a Christian in My Heart." A

Joint worship service with 15th Avenue Baptist Church, February 22, 1971.

fellowship followed in which we all became better acquainted. We parted with everyone agreeing that this had to be an annual occasion. When we got home that night, our entire family declared that the day had been a wonderful time of worship and fellowship. When Veta and I turned in, neither of us could get to sleep. We reflected on the day and agreed that the joint services had been one of the high-water marks of our lives as Christians.

That evening all three television stations shared the story and clips of the morning worship service. The same was the case for both newspapers on Monday. *The Tennessean* gave the story the entire first page of the Local section, complete with pictures. All the coverage was positive and encouraged other churches to hold interracial services as well. The *Nashville Banner*, the evening paper, likewise commended both congregations, saying, "Efforts like this can be useful to establish a better understanding and relationships between Nashvillians." Enoch and I shared on the phone that we felt like the services had been worth all the trouble. We planned to do them again the following year.

In April 1971 we retired the $300,000 note on the meetinghouse that the church borrowed in 1955 to underwrite the construction. With the church free of debt, we could plan for additional, much-needed education space. At one of the deacons' meetings, David Turner proposed an interesting idea: "I'm for more space, yet every time a church builds nowadays, they spend all their money on themselves. How would it be if we find a mission project and not only build for ourselves but build for others?" His suggestion caught us by surprise, but the more we discussed the proposal, the better it sounded. So, what would the mission project be?

Kathleen Horrell, an active Woodmont member, was on the board of the Tennessee Baptist Children's Homes, a ministry of the Tennessee Baptist Convention. The TBCH was in the process of converting their housing, for children who were unable to live in their own homes due to extenuating circumstances, from dormitory style to cottage style throughout the state. Kathleen's husband, Henry, suggested, "Men, how about we build the home in Franklin? It would accommodate ten children and two houseparents. The home itself will cost $75,000, and Kathleen and I will furnish it." The church enthusiastically received the idea, and the wheels started turning. We completed the home in June 1972 and joyfully celebrated with an open house event.

The year moved along quite well. In the summer we hired Dwayne Zimmer as our minister of education. His hiring coincided with a tremendous need in our church for new education space. Dwayne was well-equipped to guide us through this planning process.

We had a youth retreat in Gatlinburg at the Wafloy Lodge in December. It was raining to beat the band. The guys said, "Dr. Sherman, we gotta have our annual youth retreat football game." I replied, "Have you guys looked outside? The weather is chilly and raining." That did not slow them down a bit, so we had a football game in the rain for about an hour. Thankfully, no one broke any bones, and we had a ton of fun. Of course, that night after taps, we chased kids all over the place and did not get to sleep until about 1:30 a.m. The next morning at 7:00 a.m., Sunny Zimmer, our new minister of education's wife, took a pan and spoon and walked through the girls' and guys' quarters beating the pan. She said, "If you all are going to keep us up at night, I'm paying you back with the same medicine in the morning." Later, we laughed about Sunny's antics. As a mid-town church, we had young people from seven different high schools. The youth retreat really did bring our young people closer to Christ and to each other. The retreat became a yearly event.

We planned the new Education Building in 1972 and built it in 1973 at a cost of $352,000. To underwrite the new building, our finance committee came up with a new angle. Instead of floating a loan with a bank and paying interest in a conventional way, we proposed to borrow money from our church members and pay them the interest. We called the program WIN—Woodmont Investment Now. The idea caught on. Folks loaned us their money, and we wrote them promissory notes with interest rates with the date they had given the loan. Our members then made a WIN pledge for three years, pledging to give a specified amount each month over and above their tithes. These gifts would retire the notes.

Woodmont had accomplished several milestones in our first five years. Nearly eight hundred people had united with the church, and the television ministry was reaching forty to fifty thousand each Sunday. The budget had increased, which allowed us to retire the debt for the meetinghouse. Mission offerings had grown, and we were able to build a house for the Tennessee Baptist Children's Home. We had a lot to be thankful for as we began 1973.

On the home front Donny had matured from a fifth grader to a tenth-grade high schooler. Like his old man, Donny began playing trombone in the fifth grade. In sixth grade he played quarterback on a junior pro football team, which Bill Smith and I coached, that won the city championship. In ninth grade at West Middle School, he was the quarterback on the team that also won the city championship. I enjoyed coaching Donny's basketball team as well. He was a fine player. We won our league but lost in the championship. In high school Donny began singing in the youth choir at church.

Debbie was a second grader and a straight A student at Wood-mont Elementary when we came to Nashville. Before long she began to play the clarinet in the school band. She was a member of Girls in Action (GAs) at church and sang in the children's choir. As a seventh grader she was bused across town to Washington Junior High School where she became a cheerleader. She related well to all her schoolmates, most of whom were African American. Almost every night she would spend an hour or more on the phone tutoring some of her friends. We were all mighty proud of her.

Family picture in Nashville, Christmas, 1971.

David was five when we came to Woodmont. He went to first grade at Woodmont Elementary, following in his brother's and sister's footsteps. He was a people person, like his siblings, and enjoyed his schoolmates. In the fourth grade he also began to play the trombone. He was in children's choir at church and became a Royal Ambassador, a boys' missionary ministry. He became a Christian when he was eight years old. I had the joy of baptizing all three of our children. Our kids got along about as well as any family. Veta and I truly enjoyed being parents. Yes, there were times when they tried our patience, yet the good times far outnumbered the aggravating ones.

Veta and I began to play tennis for recreation and fellowship. We sometimes played on Sunday afternoons with church members. I also played church slow-pitch softball. I began as a short fielder since I still had good speed; however, as the years went by, I switched to pitcher. We had some fine teams over the years. In fact, we played for the city championship on three occasions. One night James Collins, an African American member of our church, climbed into the van and moved to the back row. I was driving. I said, "James, come up here and ride shotgun. I'm not going to drive this van with you sitting in the back row." He knew that we all loved and accepted him.

After the first five years we were thankful that God had called us to Woodmont and Nashville. We had become inTexacated Tennesseans!

9
SOME SCARY MOMENTS AT WOODMONT

1973–1977

Our church was looking forward to the construction of a new education building in 1973. After thirty-seven years in the old building, we needed the space. As pastor I have observed that new facilities generate a new enthusiasm in the congregation by sending a signal that things are happening. We dedicated the building, which was located between the meetinghouse and chapel, in the fall. Classrooms for our children in first through sixth grades were on the ground level. The second level held new office space for our staff as well as a lovely parlor and church library. The third level housed a new Sunday School department for our growing college ministry.

The house that previously served our college department now became a missionary house. Our men spruced it up over several Saturdays. The Howard Stevens family was the first to occupy the house; they served as missionaries in Mexico. The missionary house put flesh and blood to the Great Commission and hearing the stories of what missionaries did firsthand was a blessing to our congregation.

An interesting baptism occurred on the first Sunday night in December 1973. During the winter months the church heated the water in the baptistry. Unbeknownst to me, the pilot light to the heating element had blown out on this particular evening. Although the pump continued to circulate the water, it remained unheated. We had two candidates to baptize—Muffin Roper, the daughter of one of our deacons, and a young man who was a musician. I entered the baptistry during a hymn. Even though I was wearing waders, the water was so cold I could hardly breathe. At that time, I should have explained the situation to the congregation and postponed the baptism; however, I was not that quick on my feet. By the time the hymn was complete, I was literally shaking. My voice quivered as I quoted the Great Commission. I turned to Muffin, who looked angelic in her robe, and whispered, "It's a little cool." She shrugged her shoulders and started down the steps. Her foot hit the frigid water, and her expression turned to one of terror. With each step down she made a horrendous face until she came into view of the congregation. Her face then became like that of an angel. I controlled my laughter. I prayed a short prayer and immersed her. She was trembling all over. Afterwards, she turned and in TWO LEAPS cleared seven stairs to stand on the landing. I then turned to the young musician who stood on the other landing. He shrugged his shoulders and started down the steps. His experience was the same as Muffin's had been. I prayed another short prayer and immersed him. He, too, made a quick exit. I prayed a short prayer and hastily left the pool. As I entered the dressing room, the musician opened the door of his changing stall and said, "Pastor, if you had let me make several rounds in the pool, I would have been ready for it." Such was the most unusual baptism I ever experienced.

In 1972 Blanton Hall, which housed 80 percent of the faculty at Belmont College, burned. Belmont's president, Dr. Herbert Gabhart, served as the interim pastor at Woodmont before I came on the scene. Our church made a $30,000 commitment to the college to help meet their needs, giving the first $5,000 in June 1974.

The year 1974 moved along smoothly until August. In each church that we served, Veta and I invited the deacons and their wives to a homemade ice cream gathering at our house for the August meeting. The folks came with their freezers, and we met outside on our driveway. Following the business, we ate ice cream until the world was level. Life does not get any better than that—a good time of feasting and fellowship! A little past 9:00 p.m. everyone went home, and we turned in after the 10:00 p.m. news.

About 12:30 a.m. somebody began pounding on our back door, shouting, "Dr. Sherman! Dr. Sherman! Your church is on fire!" I came out of the bed, taking all the cover with me, and bolted to the back door. Two of Donny's high school friends had driven by the church and noticed flames leaping through the chapel's roof. I asked, "Have you called the fire department?" They answered, "Yes." By this time Veta was out of bed and putting on her clothes. We quickly drove the six blocks to the church. By the third block we could smell smoke. We rounded the corner and saw flames leaping through the chapel's roof. Four fire trucks were already there. The scene was frenetic as the firemen tried to keep the fire from spreading to the rest of our facilities. I parked the car and ran to unlock the doors for the firemen. They were able to contain the fire to the chapel; however, the doors to our education building and meetinghouse were left open, and smoke poured throughout our entire church facility. When the smoke settled, every piece of furniture, carpet, and floor was as black as asphalt.

The firemen spent over two hours trying to control the flames. Later that night the fire chief and I walked through most of the buildings with a flashlight. The chapel looked like a church from England during World War II. Amongst the fire damage was a broken window and a path of beer bottles strewn down the hall which led to the investigators labeling the fire as arson. As soon as church members heard of the blaze, they began coming by the scores. Folks just shook their heads and openly wept. I did too. I remained at the church until daybreak and then returned home to eat breakfast, take a shower, and change my smoke-filled clothes only to return to church about 7:30 a.m. One fire truck was still there to extinguish a small fire that had broken out again in the chapel. I could hardly breathe as I walked down the halls; the smell of smoke was stifling. I went into my office to get the number of the insurance company and saw that the mat on my desk had melted.

The insurance agent had already heard about the fire and said that he could send two men to clean up the buildings. I told him that he perhaps should see the extent of the fire and smoke damage. I reminded him that we had a television service to air in five days. He was respectful but said that was all that he could promise. I asked if our people would come and clean all the facilities, save the chapel, would the insurance company pay each member minimum wage for the hours worked? He replied, "Yes." I thanked him and told him that we would keep an honest record.

I immediately called all three television stations and asked them to please put out an appeal for our church members to come to the church at 1:00 p.m. ready to work. All three stations graciously agreed. Jud Collins, moderator of the "Noon Show" on WSM, "must-see" TV in Nashville at that time, announced the appeal. The other stations did the same. All our members heard about the fire by Tuesday midmorning. I went home and grabbed a two-hour nap and headed back to the church at noon.

When I pulled into the parking lot, I was amazed. It looked like an ant bed with folks working all over the place. Many of them had not done their housework in years, but they had the church furniture spread across the lot and were cleaning it to beat the band. They looked at me and said in jest, "Hey, Preacher, where have you been?" With that, the cleanup began. We had a senior adult keep a record of each person who worked and how many hours he or she worked. We divided up in teams and sent a team to each area of the building. We first focused on the meetinghouse. The oak pews were as black as pitch. The tile on the floor was the same. We used a mild detergent, triple aught steel wool, and elbow grease. It was August and hot, so we opened all the windows. The air-conditioning could not be turned on, as it had to be cleaned—by professionals. Every age group, from kids to seniors, showed up to help. The Hillsboro High School football team was in two-a-day workouts. Our son, Donny, was the quarterback. He and a group of players, most of whom were not members of our church, worked for three days in between workouts. Our senior adults sat in chairs and cleaned seven thousand books in our library that week. That cleanup was the beatenest thing you have ever seen.

The work went on every day and evening all week. Several restaurants in the Green Hills Shopping Center sent suppers for us. On Wednesday night we had a brief prayer meeting and then continued working until 10:00 p.m. By Friday evening the work was done! We circled in the parking lot, held hands, and sang the Doxology. There was laughter, and there were tears. The final tab showed that 368 folks of all ages had worked on the church that week. On Friday night the pastor from Woodmont Christian Church, which was across the street, came by. He said, "Bill, I've watched your congregation this week. They have been an inspiration to me. I suspect you probably feel like you had a college education this week." I replied, "Yes, and we have paid one heck of a tuition for it."

Come Sunday we had the largest congregation that I had ever seen in morning worship. We began the service by standing and singing the Doxology. When the people sat down, we heard scores of "bump, bump." We had cleaned and waxed the oak pews so proficiently that our members almost slid from their seats. The "bumps" were from hundreds of knees hitting the pews in front of them.

When I reflected upon this most unusual week, several impressions came to me. First, we had all worked ourselves to death, yet no one complained. Second, the fire created a genuine revival of interest and focus for us. Third, while the fire was not a good thing in itself, God used the fire for good. Folks showed up that I had scarcely seen in worship. The work that we did turned the experience into one of ownership—while this is God's church, it is also MY church. The whole event turned out to be a blessing in disguise, as Romans 8:28 states: "And we know that in all things God works for the good of those who love him, who have been called according to his purpose" (NIV). Now the congregation had to decide whether to rebuild the chapel or build a Christian life center. The decision became a lively and potentially divisive question.

One Saturday morning we had an outdoor workday at church. About thirty answered the call. Our church buildings were on one of the busiest corners in Nashville—Woodmont and Hillsboro Road. Over ten thousand cars went through this intersection every day, so we wanted to have everything looking sharp. Steve Horrell and I were going to trim a large bodark tree in the front yard of our missionary house. Some of the tree limbs were so low that they interfered with mowing. Chainsaw in hand, I scaled the ladder about fifteen feet. While Steve held the ladder, I jokingly said, "Tell my wife I died a brave man." When the limb I was working on fell to the ground, it coiled up and kicked directly back to the ladder. Steve instinctively stepped aside. The limb hit the ladder like a battering ram, slammed into my face, and pushed the ladder upright. I had the presence of mind to throw the chainsaw away as I hit the ground with such force that I bounced three times.

I struggled to breathe and began to roll back and forth as what felt like volts of electricity surged through my body. Steve rushed to me and said, "Dr. Sherman, Dr. Sherman, don't move." I replied, "Steve, I can't help it." This continued for about ten or fifteen seconds. Then the electricity faded, and I began to feel pain. I had broken my left leg, dislocated my foot, and fractured my wrist. My back was burning as well. At the hospital we learned that I had fractured my T12 vertebra. Dr. Mike Seshul, our deacon chairman, came to the hospital on Saturday afternoon and said, "Pastor, you have an impressive array of injuries." Months later we laughed about his words. I was in the hospital for two weeks.

I came home wearing a back brace with a full leg cast on my left leg. I was thankful to be home. The membership was so kind, sending cards, gifts, candy, and so forth. As pastor I was always the one giving, but now I was the one receiving, which was an awkward situation for me. Days passed, and I began to walk a bit on crutches. When I did, however, my foot turned blue, and my leg felt immense pressure. I shared this description with Mike, as he was a radiologist at Baptist Hospital. We went to the hospital for a test to see if I had sustained a blood clot. When Mike came in with the report, I could tell the news was not good. He shared that I had sustained a nineteen-inch blood clot in my femoral vein. The clot started below my left knee and extended up until the vein entered my abdomen. The atmosphere shifted to one of soberness as I was immediately taken to the ICU. I had to keep my leg elevated to twelve inches above my heart, and a nurse had to sit bedside with me. I received around-the-clock IV Heparin to dissolve the clot.

About 1:00 a.m. Dr. Wally Wheelhouse came to my bed. I was still awake. He shared, "Dr. Sherman, I don't want to scare you; however, I have looked at your chart, and I just want to say if there is anything in this world you need to tend to, you need to do it now." I looked at him and said, "Doc, I took care of that a long time ago. I have my druthers. I'd druther wake up in this bed in the morning, as I do not wish to leave my family and friends. But if God has another plan for me, that will be all right, too." He looked at me, nodded his head up and down, and said, "Well, I just felt like I should let you know where you are medically." I thanked him. For the next eight days I remained in ICU; then I moved to room 8127 for two more weeks before coming home. When I rode into the driveway I was singing, "Gee It's Good to Be Back Home Again!" From that moment on I never took God, my life, my family, or my friends for granted. I had missed ten weeks in the pulpit. It was good to get back.

The question looming over the congregation in 1975 was what to do about the chapel? The insurance company had given us a good settlement. We simply had to come to a decision. There were two groups, each of which was quite passionate in its feelings. One wanted to restore the chapel. The other wanted to raze the chapel and build a Christian life center. Advocates from each group had visited my office asking me to lobby for their cause. We announced a meeting that would gather on a Wednesday night in the meetinghouse, strictly following the one-month notice required by the bylaws. The saints gathered. The dilemma we faced was how to keep unity of spirit. As any pastor knows, the church cannot move forward if a large percentage of the membership is upset. Fortunately, the chairman of the deacons was our moderator, not the pastor. After an opening hymn I spoke briefly. "Friends, we are here to resolve the question of what to do concerning the chapel. There are those among us who would like to replace it; others among us wish to go in another direction. Whatever we do, let's express ourselves with Christian manners. Please share your viewpoint in three to four minutes so that all who wish to speak will be able to do so. After the vote, may we join hands and hearts that we fulfill God's purpose for this congregation on this corner. In short, may we 'fight like Christians and get on with it.'" A spirited discussion followed; however, everyone kept his cool. After forty-five minutes we voted. The vote was 70 percent to rebuild and 30 percent for a Christian life center.

The Chapel Renovation Committee ran with the ball. The design called for the worship space to be turned around with the platform in front of a beautiful stained glass window. Since the fire had destroyed the original stained glass windows, the Bob Fulcher family came forward and provided funds for new ones in honor of his father's family who were charter members in 1941. There would also be a balcony that would seat an additional one hundred people. The work moved forward at midyear, and we completed the chapel in spring 1976. Twenty-five percent of our total church offerings for the year went to Christian missions.

During these years our children continued to stay busy. Donny graduated from Hillsboro High School in May 1975. He served as quarterback for the Burros all three years. He lettered two years in basketball. He ran track all three years of high school as well. The mile relay team won the city championship in 1974 and 1975. The 1975 team came in third in the state. He sang in the Glee Club and in the quartet when they presented *The Music Man* his senior year. As a parent, being a part of his activities was a joy. One experience that stands out in my memories from Donny's senior year was on a Friday evening in May 1975. The family was gathered around the table playing Rook. Debbie turned to Donny and said, "Donny, isn't this the night of your senior prom?" He replied, "Yes." I turned to him and said, "Son, why didn't you get a date and go?" He answered, "Well, I didn't have the sweets on any girl. I'd rather just be here playing Rook with y'all." That warmed his parents' hearts. He entered the University of Tennessee at Martin on a football scholarship that fall.

Chapel fire at Woodmont, Fall of 1974.

Restored Woodmont Chapel, Spring of 1976.

Debbie was in middle school from 1972 through 1975. She was also an outstanding athlete. During the seventh grade, she was bussed to Washington Junior High School where she was a cheerleader. The next two years she attended West Junior High School where she excelled in basketball and track. She was a guard in basketball and ran the 880-yard race and mile relay in track. We kept busy taking in all her sporting events.

David was in elementary school during these years. There were no organized sports events, but he did play junior pro football on Saturdays and basketball on the church team. He played trombone in the band at school. He, like his older brother and sister, was in the middle of activities at church—RAs, children's choir, Sunday School, and Church Training. Our entire family attended each of the kids' activities. Being a parent was a busy but fun time.

In February 1976 we began a children's worship service for children who were four years old through second grade. They sat with their parents in the meetinghouse and left for their lesson during offering time.

Our youth group went to Chicago that summer to lead a Vacation Bible School and revival in a small Baptist church. Debbie was in the group and came home higher than a kite with spiritual enthusiasm. Later that summer a bizarre event happened after Sunday evening worship.

As our evening service concluded and I had shaken hands with everyone, I walked to the center of the meetinghouse to pick up my Bible. Two men approached me—one was short and wearing a leather jacket and the other was tall and dressed to do yard work. The short one said, "Dr. Sherman, we need to talk to you in private. Could we go to your office?" I had an eerie feeling about the situation. I walked to the side of the front pews and said, "Fellas, this is private enough. What do you have on your minds?" There were still about twenty people lingering in the church house. The short man said, "Sir, my partner and I are detectives. We have been informed that your church is going to be robbed later tonight. We are going to stay and apprehend the robbers." I responded, "If you are detectives, where are your credentials?" He reached into his pocket and pulled out his wallet. There was his picture with words below that read, "Detective of the Los Angeles Police Department." I asked, "If you are detectives for the L.A. Police Department, what are you doing here?" He replied, "Ahh, we are on special assignment." This whole thing just did not mesh. Further, the tall man reeked of booze. I said, "If you are a detective, why are you drinking on the job?" He squirmed and replied, "Ahh, I've only had one beer." The situation was getting tense. I said, "Guys, this just doesn't add up. If you will go downtown and bring back an officer from the Nashville Police Department to verify your story, we will talk further. Otherwise, thanks, but no thanks." The men turned red in the face and replied, "You mean you are going let somebody rob this church?" I said, "Guys, this is it." They turned and walked slowly up the aisle to the back of the church. I stood there wondering what, if anything, would come of it. The church members who were present had taken this all in. One of our deacons came rushing up to me and asked, "Pastor, who are those guys?" I told him that I did not know. He said, "I'll follow them out and make sure they leave the property." I replied, "That's a good idea." Wayne Robbins came up to me and asked, "What was that all about?" I said, "Wayne, we might ought to go see about our deacon. I don't want those guys to do something to him." We walked up the aisle and looked out the front door. All was clear. About this time a police car sailed into our parking lot off Woodmont and drove at breakneck speed up to where we were standing. I waved him down, but before I could say anything, the officer said, "You have just been robbed!"

The two men who approached me were criminals from Florida. They also had a female accomplice. A week before they robbed a church on a Sunday night in Bradenton, Florida. Folks in Florida got their license number as they left the church. An officer stopped them in Georgia, but they escaped, wounding the officer in the process. They came to Nashville where they robbed a motel the next Saturday night. They visited a bar in Nashville on Sunday afternoon where they began making plans to rob a church that night.

The bartender overheard them and notified the Nashville Police Department. A SWAT team rushed to the bar and tailed them as they drove off. When the robbers saw the lights on at our church, they parked the car on the street behind the church, leaving the female accomplice in the car. The two men walked up Hillsboro Road, down the side of the church, and entered through the front doors while the service was still in progress. They picked up a bulletin, read my name, and waited in the foyer until we dismissed. As one of our members walked by, they asked him, "Which one of those men down there is Dr. Sherman?" This is how they knew to call me by my name. While the men were in the church, the SWAT team arrested the woman in the getaway car on Hampton. A car with four additional officers was across the street at the YMCA parking lot. Another car with three officers was on the west side of our parking lot behind the dumpster. A third car with two officers was the car that drove into our parking lot to tell me that we had been robbed. When the two men who intended to rob us left our front entrance, they ran down the east side of the building. The waiting SWAT team assumed that they *had* robbed us. All three cars came charging in, lights flashing, and microphone blaring, "Stop! Police!" The two robbers made a critical mistake then. They reached down and pulled out pistols that were taped to their legs. The officers, seeing the guns, fired their weapons, and the two men fell, seriously wounded.

All this action had taken place as Wayne and I were walking up the aisle in the church. We did not hear the guns as we were in the front of the church house, and the action transpired behind the church house. I came back into the meetinghouse to a great deal of frantic noise in the back foyer. Our resident missionary, from the missionary house, was shouting, "They shot them down! They shot them down!" I double-timed it to the foyer where an officer, the leader of the SWAT team, said, "Dr. Sherman, unfortunately we had to shoot the two men. They are outside. Would you come and identify them?" I was shocked and rushed to the parking lot. A number of our folks were there. The atmosphere was frenetic—an ambulance pulled in, two television crews were present, and some fifty or more people circled the two wounded men. Several of our church members, who were at home listening to the police band on the radio, heard, "A robbery is now in progress at Woodmont Baptist Church. Police are instructed not to fire their weapons in the buildings." The ambulance took the men to the hospital. The police asked me to come to the station and give my version of the encounter. Veta took the kids and went home. As I drove home from the station about 1:00 a.m., I realized what a tenuous situation I had faced, and I thanked the Lord for seeing us through a potentially disastrous evening. I held the family a lot tighter when I gave them hugs on Monday morning. In an interview with a reporter the next day, I shared that there is nothing dull about being a Baptist preacher.

The rest of 1976 was calmer. The Clark Scanlons, serving in Guatemala, moved into the missionary house. He had been at Baylor and Southwestern Seminary with my brother, Cecil. He and his wife, Sarah, were class folks. The Scanlons would have a remarkable influence on the future of Woodmont. In another area of ministry, we finished the year by overgiving our budget. This allowed us to give the last $10,000 of our pledge to Belmont College. The remaining funds enabled us to be involved in a mission trip that changed the mission horizon at Woodmont.

The year 1977 began well for us. Our singles ministry was growing. The superintendent of the college department had a novel idea. Many of our former college students had come back to work in Nashville. They did not quite feel comfortable with our current singles ministry, as most of the singles were ten to twenty years older; so they would come to worship but not to Sunday School. As a result, we began a "redshirt" class.[1] The idea worked! Within a month we had fifteen to twenty members on a regular Sunday. Soon we had the foundation of a sure enough young singles ministry.

---

[1]   "Redshirt" is a term frequently used in college athletics. A player who is "redshirted" is withdrawn by the coach from competition for a year in order to develop skills and extend playing eligibility for another year.

On another front, we had been getting a number of phone calls from our television congregation. Our signal reached north into southern Kentucky, south into northern Alabama, and two hundred miles both east and west of Nashville. Over one hundred thousand people viewed the Woodmont service each Sunday according to Nielsen ratings. Callers continually requested a cassette recording of the worship service. In the spring we purchased two cassette recorders that could make three copies at once. Eight of our church members came every Monday morning to copy, package, and mail the free tapes to those who requested one. For the first year or two the requests numbered forty to fifty a week; however, by 1981 there were over five hundred requests each week.

The ministry that became one of Woodmont's signature ministries came into being during winter 1977. As I was walking down the hall to prayer meeting one Wednesday evening, Clark, our resident missionary, intercepted me. He said, "Bill, do you think we could get a work crew of our men and go and rebuild a church in Guatemala?" I replied, "Clark, that's a great idea. I'll make an announcement tonight and see if the idea flies." I made the announcement, and before I could get out of the chapel, over twenty men had come up to me and said, "Count me in!" Within a week forty-two men had volunteered. Since it was untenable to send that many, we came up with a plan to send two teams. Fifteen would go one week, and fifteen would go the following week. Clark would direct the teams and be our interpreter both weeks.

This endeavor fit into the convention's emphasis known as Bold Mission Thrust, which the Southern Baptist Convention affirmed in 1976. The goal of Bold Mission Thrust was to evangelize the world by 2000. One method of achieving this was to have local churches send teams on short-term volunteer mission projects around the globe. Volunteers shared the gospel while they worked. Preparatory work for our two teams was underway. Clark led several conferences as to the "dos and don'ts" for our volunteers. One thing he emphasized: "If you are a smoker, you will not smoke on this mission. Guatemalan Christians are sticklers on this issue. We will do nothing as a team to undermine our missionaries' work." I led the first group, and our minister of education led the second group the following week. Veta's dad, Luther Cole, a lifelong carpenter, could do anything in construction—woodwork, electrical, plumbing, you name it. He gladly accepted the invitation to go. Our first team had every trade represented except a concrete mason, which was vital as the walls of the proposed church were cinder blocks. We sent out an SOS to the Nashville Baptist Association, and Floyd Fry volunteered. Floyd was a mason and a faithful member of a sister Baptist church in East Nashville.

The first group flew to Miami on Sunday, February 19, 1977, and we landed in Guatemala City that afternoon where the pastor met us. We went to evening worship at the church site where we sat in chairs or on the ground with the stars shining above us. Before our arrival workers had dug a square trench and filled it with concrete. This method is a splatter foundation, outlining where the walls will be. I preached, and Clark served as an interpreter. About halfway through my message, a man stood up and said in Spanish, "Mr. Scanlon, I want to become a believer in Jesus." Clark turned to me and said, "Bill, hold on." He turned back to the man and said in Spanish, "Sir, please come forward." Clark asked him a series of questions: "Do you believe that Jesus is the Son of God? Will you confess your sins and ask Jesus to come into your heart to forgive you? Will you follow him in baptism and live the Christian life?" To all these questions the man answered, "Sí." Clark asked him to be seated and turned to me and said, "OK, Bill, continue with the sermon." I was so mystified by what I had just witnessed that I had no idea where I was in the sermon, but, somehow, I managed to continue.

After the service Clark introduced each of our fifteen-member crew by name, vocation, and the schooling that each person had. Almost all our men had college degrees, and several had advanced degrees. After the service was over, I asked Clark why he went to such great lengths to describe our education. He said, "Bill, I did that for a reason. Many church members here feel that with a college degree they are above manual labor. I wanted these folks to know that Christians need to do whatever work is needed." After the introductions were over, we made our way across town to the small Bible college campus where we were staying.

For the next five days, twelve-hour shifts were our new normal. The middle of the day was hot. Not a living soul complained. Some folks built the scaffolding, others mixed the concrete, others handed the mud and blocks to Floyd. The walls went up. I was reminded of Nehemiah. We worked from 7:00 a.m. until dark. After dark we ate supper, showered, and hit the hay. About noon one day, Floyd, who was dripping with sweat, said, "Fellas, let me blow a minute. At my church when I told them I was going on a work crew to Guatemala, they responded, 'Aw, Floyd, you're going down there with all those brain trusts and pencil pushers from Woodmont. Why, you'll never break a sweat!'" He then sighed and said, "Guys, you all are working me to death. My union only allows me to lay four hundred blocks a day. I've counted, and we've already laid 450 blocks, and it's not even noon." We all had a good laugh. We went across the street and bought Floyd a Coca-Cola. By the end of the first week, the walls were in place. We were ready for the second crew to finish the job.

One sidebar experience that stimulated us every day was the ride across Guatemala City back and forth to the work site. The people drove like crazy folk. Clark drove our van, and we all felt like we were in the demolition derby. When approaching an intersection, everyone blew the horn and floored the gas. The first day I rode shotgun, and it shook me up. I asked Clark, "Hey, who has the right-of-way in these intersections?" He replied, "Whoever has the most guts." After the first day I rode in the back of the van and hoped and prayed the entire ride.

I flew home on Saturday so that I could preach on Sunday morning. I was filled with joy and excitement from the week. One of our deacons said, "Pastor, you took one breath this morning and preached for thirty minutes without looking at a note. You were revved up!" I really was. I was thankful that the week had gone so well. No one had gotten hurt. Everybody did his share and more. The church members provided our noon meal each day, which allowed us to get to know them. We practiced our

Spanish on them, and they practiced their English on us. This made for a lot of laughs. The second crew finished the job we had started by putting in the roof, doors, and windows. Our time in Guatemala had been a worthy investment.

A popular youth song of this era was "Pass It On." The opening words say, "It only takes a spark to get a fire going." As I reflect on our Guatemala mission trip, it was the spark that served as a catalyst to really get our mission fires burning at Woodmont. When the men came back, they were enthusiastic about missions and mission trips. On Sunday and Wednesday nights I gave any participant on the trip the opportunity to share what the experience had meant to them. Missions involvement was like the measles—it was contagious. When summer came, thirty-eight youth went to Chicago. They led Bible schools and Backyard Bible Clubs in two small Baptist churches for two weeks. Our daughter, Debbie, was in this group. She came home with a ton of stories.

Another unusual experience happened during these years. About 9:00 p.m. our telephone rang. The voice at the other end of the line screamed, "Dr. Sherman, you must help me!" The caller then shared his story. He had been in a relationship with his neighbor's wife for several years. That night she broke down and confessed to her husband in tears. The husband then came across the yard and rang the neighbor's doorbell. The husband said to him, "You have put me through hell for the past two years. I could not understand why my wife had pulled away from me. Now I am going to put you through hell. I am going to shoot you, but you do not know when it will be. I have a perfect view of your driveway. You will not know when I'm going to pull the trigger, but in the next six months it will happen. Get ready for it." He then turned and disappeared into the dark. The caller screamed into the phone once again, "Dr. Sherman, you've got to help me!" I responded as best I could and asked him if there was any way that he could apologize to his neighbor. He did not seem to think that would fly. We talked a bit further, but he remained distraught. Finally, I told him that I would pray for him. He thanked me and hung up.

Several weeks later my wife attended a church member's gathering in Seven Hills. As the conversations developed, a woman said, "We had the strangest thing happen in our neighborhood. A fine family three doors down just disappeared. They did not say anything about moving to any of us. None of us knows what happened to them. A moving van appeared about two weeks later, and I asked the driver where he was taking all the furniture. He said he was taking it to storage. That's all he knew."

Veta came home and shared the story. I said, "It may well be the family of the husband who talked to me on the phone the other night. I suppose the move happened so the man could prevent the husband from shooting him." As I have thought about the entire bizarre experience, I thank God for the merits of faithfulness in marriage. Fidelity has its own rewards.

In fall 1977 we had a lay-led revival. One night featured a men's chorus with seventy-one men in the choir led by Ray Connor. On another night two country music stars who were members of our church—George Hamilton IV and Larry Gatlin—provided the special music. Our church ministries were going well. The singles ministry was expanding. We formed a new Sunday School department uniting the redshirt class, which had grown to thirty or more, with our other two existing singles classes. Our college department was running seventy-five or more each Sunday. We were meeting our budget. The church had a good spirit. We were thankful for God's good blessings.

As the year drew to a close, the SBC elected me to the Home Mission Board. We met twice a year in Atlanta and sought to map out the best strategy to reach our nation for Christ. In November the Tennessee Baptist Convention elected me as president. I honestly did not believe I would be elected as I was not a native Tennessean nor had I attended a Tennessee Baptist college. I simply did not think the people of Tennessee knew who I was. Earl Davis, pastor of First Baptist Church, Memphis, made the nomination. Rather than focus on me, he shared about Woodmont's investment in Tennessee Baptist life. Our church was third in Cooperative Program giving to state and national causes in the state convention. He also talked about our mission trips and the television ministry. After the vote, much to my surprise, I was elected. Finally, Southern Baptist Seminary asked me to be a field supervisor for pastors in Middle Tennessee who were pursuing their Doctor of Ministry degrees. What a privilege. We met with a dozen or more pastors every other week at Woodmont to read and discuss their papers. There were forty-two assignments for each pastor. Our meetings proved to be a redemptive time of sharing and learning together.

The busy year closed with the church honoring Veta and me for our ten-year anniversary. Several folks shared. Then the church presented us with a generous gift of $2,000 and two additional weeks away from church duties for relaxation and travel. In those ten years, through ups and downs, we had become family. We were thankful God had led us to Woodmont.

10
WOODMONT—BATTLES ON THE OUTSIDE

1978–1982

The year 1978 was eventful for Woodmont in several ways. Our budget was now over $400,000, which meant we could employ a full-time minister of youth and singles. Our summer youth directors had served us well; however, our singles department had grown measurably. We had four Sunday School classes with attendance right at the one hundred mark each Sunday. We felt that a full-time minister could better serve the spiritual interests of both groups.

Our missionary house was always occupied. Several folks suggested that we provide a missionary apartment as well. The idea was well received, and consequently, we rented an apartment.

Another innovation proved very helpful to our office staff. Open-heart surgery was becoming more commonplace, and a dozen or so men in our congregation had the surgery. In each case, our folks called the church office by the score to get a report on the outcome, which interrupted the work of our church secretary. She spent so much time talking on the phone that she could hardly get her work done. We solved the problem by adding another phone line that we called WBIS or Woodmont Baptist Information Service. Each morning we recorded a brief overview of ministry activities for the day as well as who was in the hospital, who was recovering from surgery, and how he or she was faring. We could convey other pertinent information when necessary, such as when the youth would arrive home from retreats or mission trips. The phone line was a wise investment and much appreciated by the office personnel.

Donny, quarterback
for the University of
Tennessee, Martin,
1978.

Participation in mission trips increased in 1978. Fourteen individuals or groups from Woodmont went to the Dominican Republic, Ghana, South Korea, and Guatemala. Fifty youth went to Chicago and worked in four different churches, conducting Vacation Bible Schools and Backyard Bible Clubs. Dwayne Zimmer took five men to Midlothian, Illinois, to do construction work and hold a revival. All told, seventy church members served on mission trips.

As the year drew to a close, we reached our budget and met the goals of our home and foreign mission offerings. We had new members and a full staff in place to serve them. The year ended with Woodmont hosting the Tennessee Baptist Convention.

On the home front Donny was playing quarterback for UT-Martin. George McIntyre, who had been on the Vanderbilt football staff and a deacon at Woodmont, was his coach. We made the two-and-a-half-hour drive to each home game, arriving back in Nashville about 1:00 a.m. Donny was also on the dean's list, which pleased us.

Debbie was a senior at Hillsboro in 1978. Her peers voted her Most Athletic Girl in the senior class. She ran cross-country in the fall. In the winter she made all-city guard in basketball. And in the spring, she ran the 880 and mile relay in track. Our entire family enjoyed taking in her events. Unfortunately, she pulled her hamstring the week of the state meet and was unable to run. It was a real downer. Regardless, she gave us plenty of thrills through the years. One experience stands out. In a meet at McGavock High School, Debbie and another rival were in a close race. Around the last curve Debbie faded and came in second. Donny had come home to see her run. She was distraught as we rode home in the car. No one said anything for miles. Finally, Donny said, "Well, Debbie, were you saying, 'Are you running with me, Jesus?' on the home stretch?"[1] I wondered if that might start World War III. Debbie paused and replied glibly, "No, Donny, I was saying, 'My God, my God, why hast thou forsaken me?'" We all burst into laughter and still laugh about the story now whenever we reminisce.

David was in middle school at Montgomery Bell Academy. He played football, church basketball, and was a high jumper in track. Like his older brother and sister, he was athletic. He also played the trombone like his old man. David was plugged into all the youth activities at church as well. He was a fine son. Between church, school, and family activities, there was never a dull moment in the Sherman house.

Two significant telephone calls occurred in 1978. The Tennessee chapter director of the Football Hall of Fame called in the spring. He said, "Dr. Sherman, our chapter has voted unanimously for you and Mayor Bredesen to receive our Distinguished American Award this October. We will make the presentation at the fall banquet." I was surprised and appreciative. My kids laughed and said, "Dad, we could understand your receiving the

---

[1]   *Are You Running With Me, Jesus?* was a bestselling book of prayers published in 1965 by American Episcopal priest and author Malcolm Boyd. Boyd was active in the civil rights movement and the anti-Vietnam War movement.

Bill and Veta at their 10th anniversary as pastor and wife.

award if it was an Extinguished Award. But we don't know about this Distinguished Award." They always kept me humble.

The second call was from Dr. A.V. Washburn, the secretary (president) of the Baptist Sunday School Board. He said, "Bill, it has come to my attention that your mother and father have served in the junior Sunday School department at the Polytechnic Baptist Church for over one hundred combined years. Is that right?" I replied, "Yes, Dr. Washburn. They married in 1926 and began working with juniors in 1928. Mother was the superintendent; Dad led the singing, completed the records and was a substitute teacher for all those years." He said, "That record is worthy of recognition. I am going to make a plaque and personally present it to them." He told me not to mention it to my parents. A month or so later I received a call from Mom and Dad one Sunday afternoon. Dr. Washburn had presented the recognition plaque before the Poly congregation that morning. Mom and Dad were deeply moved. I really appreciated what Dr. Washburn had done. Until this day I can sing the first verse of "Our Best" by memory, the song that Dad always had us sing to begin Sunday School. Those are precious memories.

In January 1979 the White House invited Veta and me to President Carter's Prayer Breakfast. Bishop Fulton J. Sheen, the featured speaker, delivered a fine message. We had the privilege of meeting President and Mrs. Carter, who were as down to earth and genuine as could be. On the flight home we both commented that neither of us ever believed that we would have such an experience. We were thankful that President Carter and his wife were affirming believers without apology.

The singles ministry at Woodmont was thriving as was our music program. With over sixty people in the choir each Sunday morning, our music ministry had outgrown the choir room. We cranked up the wheels and built a lovely new choir suite, attaching it to the back of the meetinghouse more than doubling the music space. We turned the old choir room into the music library.

Thirteen individuals or groups from Woodmont participated in mission trips to Columbia, Japan, and South Korea in 1979. Forty-eight of our youth went to Dauphin, Alabama, to lead a Vacation Bible School and a revival in a small Baptist church.

Channel 5, the CBS affiliate in Nashville, had a colorful personality named Stan Siegel. The town never knew what he would come up with next. Out of the clear blue, I received a telephone call from Stan. He said, "Dr. Sherman, I have asked Madalyn Murray O'Hair (a well-known atheist) to come to town to debate one of our preachers. She's going around the country trying to put down Christianity. I've heard you preach, and I think you can hold your own. I want you to be that preacher. I'll be the emcee. I'll give both of you equal time. What do you think? Will you participate?" I told him that I would. He said, "Great, I'll get back with you." I pretty much knew what I was facing. I had heard Madalyn debate Dr. Criswell, pastor of First Baptist Church, Dallas, several weeks earlier. Her tactics were to interrupt, to be rude, to be aggressive, and to never stop talking. This approach so frustrated Dr. Criswell that he finally shouted, "Will you please shut her up!" Madalyn then turned to the camera and said something to the effect of, "See, look how this so-called Christian is treating me. He is supposed to be a person of love." I told Veta, "No matter how pejorative she may get, I will not lose my cool."

The big night came. We all met an hour and a half before the program in Stan's office. Madalyn was disheveled in dress, and she complained constantly. I tried to carry on a civil conversation with her but was unsuccessful in my attempts. I sensed that the way she got attention was to claim that she is America's foremost atheist; otherwise, no one would give her the time of day. I truly felt sorry for her. She was not aggressive or in attack mode in Stan's office. However, that approach changed once the debate began. When the cameras starting rolling, she came out of her shell.

Stan introduced the program and the guests. He then turned and said, "Who would like to begin?" Madalyn came out of chute number four on Midnight like she was at the rodeo. She said, "Dr. Sherman, I am America's foremost atheist. I know all the arguments for the existence of God—the teleological argument, the cosmological argument, the argument from intuitive religious experience. I can push all those arguments down. The burden of proof is on your shoulders. You must convince me that there is a God!" With that, she sat back in her chair, took a deep breath, and looked at me with a smirk. I calmly replied, "Madalyn, I did not come to the station to convince anyone that there is a God. I came to give witness to the experience I have had with Jesus Christ that has turned my life around. He has given me forgiveness, a reason to live, and the power to cope with all that life can throw at me." She countered, "I don't like that word 'witness.'" I replied, "Well, this is what my life is—a witness for Jesus Christ." She snapped, "I don't even believe that Jesus Christ was an historic figure. You must prove that to me." I countered, "I can prove that Jesus Christ was an historic figure as well as you can prove Napoleon was an historic figure." She snapped, "That is nonsense. People saw Napoleon." I answered, "People saw Jesus." She countered,

"People wrote books about Napoleon." I replied, "People wrote books about Jesus." She said, "I doubt your sources!" I answered, "I doubt your sources!" She sighed and changed her approach.

She said, "Well, all Christians are hypocrites. They never have and never will live up to their claims." I countered, "Madalyn, are you aware of what Christians have done for this country? Eight out of ten universities in this country were founded by Christians in the first one hundred years of this nation. Christians have started hospitals, orphanages, and union missions in all our major cities to feed and care for the downtrodden. By the way, how many colleges, hospitals, orphanages, and union missions have atheists started and maintained? Name one." She was silent.

About this time our emcee asked if any persons in the gallery had questions. Several preachers present challenged Madalyn on various points. When the dialogue finished and the cameras quit rolling, Madalyn left in a hurry. She did not speak to anyone. Jack Spence, a deacon at Woodmont, came up to me and said, "Preacher, this has been a good evening. If I had not been a believer and had witnessed all this, I would go away a believer. She was arrogant, disruptive, and rude. You maintained control and were respectful. By just taking in the spirit of the two of you, I would want to be like you and not her." I thanked Jack for his words. The truth of the matter was I was emotionally extended. Having all that thrown at me was difficult. Debating Mrs. O'Hair was one of the most unusual experiences of my entire ministry.

Little did I know that I would not only be fighting atheists this year but fellow Baptists as well. The annual meeting of the Southern Baptist Convention was in Houston, Texas. The messengers elected Dr. Adrian Rogers, of Memphis, Tennessee, president on the first ballot. No president in recent memory had ever been so elected. Traditionally, several candidates would be presented, then there would be a runoff between the two who received the largest number of votes. The question to be answered was, how did Adrian win on the first ballot? A movement had begun, engineered by Judge Paul Pressler, Paige Patterson, W.A. Criswell, and Adrian Rogers, who called themselves biblical conservatives.

They had quietly networked under the radar to have more messengers than ever before at the convention in Houston. Their first goal was to elect the president. Then the president would be able to appoint three persons to stack two key committees—the Committee on Committees and the Committee on Boards. These two committees are critical because they name the persons who will serve on the boards of the seminaries, boards, and agencies. So, if you elect a president for ten years who will then select like-minded people to serve on the committees, boards, and agencies, you will have FULL CONTROL of the SBC. How did they pull this off? By going throughout the land telling grassroots Baptists that we have liberals teaching in our seminaries who do not believe in the Virgin Birth, nor in the Blood, nor the Blessed Hope! These statements were lies. These men called themselves conservatives and branded all who disagreed with them moderates. This confrontation began in 1979 and lasted for ten years. These so-called conservatives were, in reality, fundamentalists. What they claimed to be a theological fight was in reality an unvarnished takeover.

I do not wish to elaborate on this ten-year battle as that is not the purpose of this book. If you wish to gain a clear understanding of what went on in the SBC, I recommend that you read my brother Cecil's autobiography, *By My Own Reckoning*. He sets forth two chapters that will set the record straight. However, I will add a few additional thoughts. Cecil and I were and are as Baptist as one can be. We believe everything that Baptists have ever believed— God, Man, Christ, the Holy Spirit, Scripture, you name it. In fall 1980 a group of moderate pastors met in Gatlinburg, Tennessee, to discuss mounting an organized opposition to the fundamentalist movement. Our group affirmed that several ruinous things would happen in the SBC if the fundamentalists succeeded. First, the world mission endeavor would suffer. Second, our seminaries would be disparaged. Third, our Sunday School board would be dismantled. Fourth, fellowship in the SBC would be destroyed. Tragically, all of the above happened. Denominationally the 1980s were a time of disparagement of one of the finest denominations in the world. Thankfully, the fundamentalists never gained control of the crown jewel—Baylor University, which was protected by the shrewd work of Texas Baptists. Veta and I are overjoyed that Baylor remains a true Baptist institution today.

Woodmont had a lot of momentum as we entered 1980. We were fully staffed in all our ministries, and our numbers were increasing in all areas of church life. The church budget was $650,000, and we had overgiven for the last five years. The singles ministry doubled in three years with over 150 singles in regular attendance. The church choir was increasing with folks filling the choir each Sunday. The television ministry continued to grow with the Nielsen rating reported at over two hundred thousand folks worshiping with us each Sunday morning.

A bright spot in 1980 was the volunteers who went overseas to do mission work. Veta and I led a group to Jamaica for Vacation Bible Schools and revivals. In addition, we had members in Granada, Mexico, and South Korea. Our choir members travelled to Mexico where they sang all the songs in Spanish. During the trip they were invited to sing a concert at a university in Mexico City. When they finished their selections, both secular and sacred, a voice in the auditorium requested "The Hallelujah Chorus." Howard Stevens, missionary to Mexico, said the person may have requested the song just to embarrass the choir. Ironically, the choir had practiced it in rehearsals and performed the song impeccably. They brought the house down. In addition to those who served overseas, we had church members serving in Washington, D.C., Puget Sound, Washington State, and Illinois. During this time our church built a second Habitat for Humanity house. Finding a team of builders, both men and women, for such a cause was never hard, and the work was rewarding. We had built both houses in North Nashville for African American families. As pastor, I always had the joy of giving the homeowners the keys to their new house. I was thankful that our members participated and showed up in good numbers for the ceremony.

Another bright spot this year was taking a group from our church to see the Passion Play in Oberammergau, Germany.

From 1634 to the present, the villagers have performed the Play every ten years. When the Black Plague was sweeping across Bavaria in the seventeenth century, members of the village at Oberammergau made a pledge to God that if He would spare their town, they would do something worthy to show their gratitude. That something became the Passion Play. The cast members are town citizens. The Play tells the story of the last week of Jesus' life including the Crucifixion and the Resurrection. The Play lasts most of the day. Though the performers speak in German, audience members can follow along with a folder in their respective language. The Play was remarkable, inspiring, and the highlight of our tour that year.

The year 1981 proved to be the finest year that Woodmont had experienced to date. Our Sunday School attendance topped the nine-hundred mark, with the high-water mark being 981 in December. Our singles had grown by 61 percent in the previous two years, and we now had six singles' Sunday School classes. Our total church membership exceeded 2,300 members. We purchased a two-story house adjacent to our property and called it Woodmont West. Our budget was $700,000. We had overgiven our budget for the seven previous years.

In 1981 the spark that the 1977 trip to Guatemala lit became a roaring fire. Woodmont members participated in twenty-one volunteer mission trips both at home and abroad. Twenty-eight people went to ten countries—Brazil, Chile, Honduras, India, Jordan, Japan, Panama, South Korea, Republic of Upper Volta, and Venezuela. An additional ninety-five people volunteered for stateside work in Michigan, Arizona, New York, and East Tennessee. All this mission involvement paid dividends in our Lottie Moon offering. In five years, our giving increased from $16,000 to $49,000. We had a doctor and his wife, Dewey and Bobbie Dunn, who inspired and personified mission volunteer work. He and Bobbie spent every vacation doing mission work. As of 2021 the two have gone on short-term medical mission trips over two hundred times. They taught a singles' class in Sunday School and urged every member to go and serve Christ in this way. Scores did. The Dunns are the personification of what two people can mean to the cause of Christ through missions.

One Saturday morning in 1981 the phone rang. On the other end was Dr. Bill Ford, a dentist in our congregation who had just returned from two weeks in Honduras. I welcomed him home and asked, "How was your trip?" He said, "Pastor, I have a story to tell you, and then I want to ask a favor." I said, "Great, shoot." He shared, "This past week in Honduras, Dr. David Harms, the missionary doctor whom I work with, shared a story. A ten-year-old girl in his town, Alva Consquela, has a life-threatening medical problem. Her heart has a hole in it and cannot pump blood as it should. If medical intervention does not occur before she grows older, she will die. I told him, 'David, let me carry her back to Nashville. We can get the operation done. Do you think her parents would let me do that?' We visited with the parents, who were overjoyed and agreed. However, there were obstacles. She had no passport; she had no visa. We prayed that these things could be overcome. We went to the airport and told the story to the clerk. The clerk said, 'I'll let you go, but you may be stopped in the States.' So Alva and I flew to New Orleans and with trepidation went through customs. I handed my passport to the officer, who looked at it and said, 'Nashville? My brother lives in Nashville. He lives in Green Hills.' I replied, 'I go to church in Green Hills, to Woodmont Baptist Church.' The officer said, 'I've driven by that church.' I said, 'Well, I have story to tell you. I've been on a mission trip to Honduras. The missionary showed me this little girl who has a hole in her heart. I've brought her back to Nashville so we can fix her heart and take her home to her parents in Honduras.' The officer said, 'I could get fired for this. How much time do you need?' I said, 'Three months.' The officer approved the proper papers, and we flew to Nashville."

Then Bill said, "Now, Preacher, here is where you come into the picture. Would you go see David Stringfield at Baptist Hospital?" (David was the hospital administrator and a church member.) "Would you tell him the story and ask him if the hospital would do the surgery for free? Then would you go to the two surgeons that have operated on so many of our members and ask them to perform the surgery for free?" I must say that I was somewhat overwhelmed by what I had heard and what he was asking for. Naturally, however, I was more than happy to perform both requests.

On Monday morning I was sitting in Stringfield's office unannounced. He was gracious and listened to my story. He leaned back in his chair, looked at the ceiling, and said, "Bill, we will do this. But you must not tell any other preacher. If you do, there will be a line of preachers around the block asking for the same thing." I told him that I would keep a lid on it. I then found the two surgeons who agreed to the plan as well. The surgery went well. Nurses who could speak Spanish volunteered to help, and a Spanish-speaking nurse stayed in Alva's room around the clock for a week. Spanish-speaking church members visited the Fords' home as long as she recuperated. Nine months later Alva came to worship. She stepped up on a box behind the pulpit and said in Spanish, "Señors, Señoras, muchas gracias," and then burst into tears. By then the entire congregation was standing, crying and cheering. Bill and Shirley Ford flew Alva back to Honduras that week and presented her to her parents—whole. Alva's case is just one example of how mission work is so fulfilling.

Another inspiring event occurred this same year. A visitor named Tommy Howard introduced himself as he left the morning service. He asked if he could come by for a visit. I told him I would welcome it. A couple of days later he came to my office. He said, "Dr. Sherman, I first heard your service on television. I am looking for a deeper meaning in my life." We continued to talk. I asked him if anyone had explained to him how to become a Christian in language that he could understand. He replied, "No." I shared the gospel with him while he listened intently. I told Him Christ would enter the life of anyone who would invite Him. He said, "I am ready." We both prayed. He looked at me with a big smile and said, "I feel better about this." I asked him if he would be comfortable coming forward and publicly affirming his faith. He replied, "Yes." He came forward the next Sunday and took his stand for Christ, and I baptized him that evening.

About a month later I was sitting in an airplane in Atlanta returning from a Home Mission Board meeting. A large gentleman sat down next to me and said, "You don't know me, but I know you. You are the pastor at Woodmont in Nashville, and I want to know something. What have you all done to Tommy Howard? He comes in Mondays on time now. He has quit gambling and drinking. He doesn't swear anymore. He is a different man. What have you done to Tommy Howard?" I told him that our church had not done anything to Tommy. However, we had introduced him to Jesus Christ; and He had made the difference. We talked all the way to Nashville. I had the joy of officiating Tommy's marriage to a fine Methodist woman. They had a wonderful life together. Tommy was an inspiration to us and a fine churchman. This is your reward as a pastor.

In 1982 our mission momentum gathered speed. We had members serving in England, Guatemala, Honduras, Indonesia, Jamaica, Mexico, Nigeria, South Korea, and Republic of Upper Volta. Others served in Colorado, Michigan, and Washington State. Some of these assignments were individuals; others were groups. Fifty choir members went to Merida, Mexico. Twenty-three church members did construction work in Guatemala. All told, ninety-four members served, plus a large group from the youth and single adults. When these folks came home, they shared how God used them, and these stories continued to inspire others.

Several new ministries began in 1982. We formed a singles' choir, another means of involving members in ministry. The group had a good sound and sang bimonthly in evening worship. We also formed a group of retired ministerial folks to answer telephone calls during morning worship. The telephone number was listed at the bottom of the screen.

Our Lottie Moon goal for 1982 was $66,000. We had a mission interest center at the front side of the meeting house displaying the goal. Dr. Dewey Dunn walked in while I was sharing the prayer calendar and quietly went by the mission display and turned the two numerals over. The Lottie Moon goal now read

$99,000. Everyone laughed, including me. When we totaled the final offering, the membership gave $100,109! As Scripture says, "O ye of little faith" (Matt 8:26 KJV). What a way to end 1982!

Donny graduated from UT-Martin in 1979. George McIntyre became the head football coach at Vanderbilt that same year and brought Donny on as the assistant coach for wide receivers. George and his family also became part of our church family at Woodmont. With their 8–3 record earning Vandy an invitation to the Hall of Fame Bowl in Birmingham, George was named National Coach of the Year by his peers. I had the privilege of leading the invocation at the celebration at the Opryland Hotel. Another highlight came in December when Donny married Tena Clower, whom he had met at church. Tena had grown up in Lebanon, Tennessee, and graduated from Tennessee Tech. The wedding took place at Woodmont, and I had the privilege of leading them in their vows. The newlyweds established a nice residence in Franklin near Nashville.

These years were Debbie's Baylor years, which she thoroughly enjoyed. During this time, she was able to go on two mission trips, including the one with Veta and me to Jamaica in 1980. We served in churches where Vinston Clementson was the pastor. He had become a Christian in 1954 when Veta and I were summer missionaries there. Debbie was also able to go to Nigeria in 1982. Her senior year she was the chairperson of Welcome Week, a time before school starts for incoming freshmen to connect with each other and the University. She made the dean's list. She was involved in Columbus Avenue Baptist Church where she led a children's choir. Debbie, like her mother, was always on the go. She graduated in 1982.

David was in middle school and high school during most of these years. He graduated from Hillsboro High School in 1981. He continued to play football and to participate in high jump, making it to the state meet. He played church basketball, was a leader in the youth choir at church, and played trombone in the band. As parents Veta and I were buzzing around taking in all the school and church activities.

Veta and I continued to play tennis each week during these years. On Tuesday nights I also played short fielder on Woodmont's slow pitch softball team. Each fall we made our annual pilgrimage to Baylor for Homecoming where we enjoyed seeing old college friends from yesteryear. Life was good.

11

WOODMONT—CHURCH LIFE

1983-1987

Something in the human spirit just appreciates hearing good news. The year 1983 began this way when the Gatlin Brothers— Larry, Steve, and Rudy—informed our church that they were giving our meetinghouse a new Yamaha grand piano and a three-manual computerized Allen organ. We were astonished and thanked them for such a generous contribution to our worship services. In addition, another Woodmont family gave new choir robes to the adult choir. How blessed we were.

Once again, we had a space problem for our educational needs, as we were running around nine hundred in Sunday School. Our singles alone now had seven classes with 259 members. What a good problem to have. We chose a committee and an architect, and, with the approval of the congregation, construction work began. We completed the space the following year, which added two floors onto the education building. We initiated another WIN program (Woodmont Investment Now), and our folks were faithful in stewardship. The new education facility enabled us to continue to grow.

For my fifteenth anniversary as pastor, the congregation graciously gave Veta and me a three-week trip to England, Scotland, and Ireland, as they knew how much I appreciated history. One of the highlights of the trip was visiting the grave of Winston Churchill, who had been such an inspiration to me. Our family listened to his speeches during World War II in the front room of our house with an old Atwater Kent radio. Another highlight of the trip was Bedford, where John Bunyan had his ministry and wrote *Pilgrim's Progress*. We worshipped at Bunyan Meeting, and following the service, a deacon kindly took us through the Bunyan Museum, which was located on church grounds. Coventry was particularly meaningful. In 1940 the Germans virtually wiped the city off the map by saturated bombings. A memorial to that dreadful night remains in the ruins of Coventry Cathedral. The Luftwaffe first dropped high explosive bombs on the city, then returned hours later and dropped incendiary bombs with the intent of burning up whatever had not been blown down. The next morning the dean walked through the rubble of the cathedral and carved onto the charred walls of the sanctuary, "Father forgive." Forgive the Germans? No. Forgive humanity for making such a colossal tragedy of human history. In Edinburgh we worshipped at the Charlotte Chapel Baptist Church. During the offertory a lady sang "Grace to You," a song composed by Mark Blankenship, our interim music director in 1975. What a small world. After a wonderful three weeks, we came home happy and weary. We found that the church had moved along very well in our absence.

Woodmont members continued to actively participate in missions in 1983, serving in Barbados, Chile, England, Gaza, Ghana, Honduras, Jamaica, Japan, Nicaragua, Costa Rica, Nigeria, Norway, Panama, Singapore, and South Korea. In addition, other members served locally in Massachusetts, Connecticut, Florida, Michigan, New Jersey, Ohio, and Tennessee. Fifty-seven members served abroad, and twenty-one, in addition to the youth group, served at home. I was amazed then, and I am amazed now when I pen these words. How did we have eighty plus members involved in short-term mission projects? First, Woodmont was a Great Commission church. Dr. West preached the message, and I continued it. The two missionary houses and missionary apartment had an influence as well. Missionaries lived among us, they preached for us, they shared inspiring stories, and they personified missions. The testimonies of church members who went on mission trips were inspiring. The people went to share the faith but found that the trip changed them as much as it changed those to whom they witnessed. Our church budget reflected the importance that missions played in our church. At the end of the year, I shared with our deacons that we had given 41 percent of our funds to ministries and missions. The actual fiscal figure was $780,000. As a church we were grateful to honor the Lord in this way.

In 1984 we were up to 1,063 in Sunday School, with even more folks attending morning worship. We had a parking problem to some degree. Woodmont Christian Church was right across the street from us. Some of our folks were parking in their parking lot and walking across the street to our church. Word came to me of the situation, and with a red face I apologized to our neighbors. I also appealed to our members. To remedy the situation, we considered adding an early worship service, which finally came to fruition in January 1985.

One meaningful area of ministry that we began several years earlier was the International Friends ministry. Women from eight Baptist churches in the area came together weekly at Woodmont to help international families adapt to American ways. Most of their husbands were in one of the many universities in the Nashville area. The gathering resembled a United Nations, with folks from all over the world participating. The ministry taught them English, how to navigate the Nashville transit system, sewing, family management, and so forth, rendering a monumental service to these internationals. The women were a long way from home and surrounded by a different culture. They welcomed having a smiling face to talk to. Each year the ministry had a dinner that they invited our staff to participate in. The women prepared a favorite dish from their countries. We would all sit down to eat, and each lady would ask if we liked her dish. I always prayed the missionary prayer before eating, "Lord, if I can get the food down, will you please keep it down?"

Our meetinghouse needed a facelift, and I asked a local painting company to give us a bid. The quote was $38,000. I had second thoughts. At that time Mr. William Jobe was our caretaker. He was much more than that—he was a fixer. William could do woodwork, plumbing, electrical, you name it, and he had a frugal streak in him like me. I invited him to my office and said, "William, would you like to be part of an adventure?" He replied, "What about?" We walked into the church house. I said, "William, I believe you and I could paint this place." His eyes got big. He asked, "How would we get to it all? These walls to the ceiling are about fifty feet." I told him I thought we could swing it by renting scaffolding, buying the paint at Hillsboro Hardware, getting drop cloths to protect the pews, and painting one section each week. He smiled and said, "Let's do it."

I touched base with our chairmen of the deacons and building and grounds. They bought in. Tom Mathias at Hillsboro Hardware said he could match the paint. We rented the scaffolding, bought brushes and rollers, and began the next Thursday afternoon. We would scaffold up the wall to the ceiling, secure the scaffold with ropes, then clean and paint. One of us would cut in, and the other would roll. Each section took about four hours. We then took the scaffolding down, placed it in a little used foyer, tied it tight, and covered it up. We did not tell anyone; we just went about our business. Hardly anyone in the membership knew what we were doing. In six months' time we finished the job and spent less than $12,000. When we announced the completion at the January deacons' meeting, two-thirds of the brethren were unaware that the transformation had even taken place. The deacons bought Mr. Jobe and me honey-baked hams for our work. We were glad to save the church about $26,000.

In 1984 we had thirty-three members go to the following countries: Belize, Brazil, Burkina Faso, Chile, Hong Kong, South Korea, Nigeria, Panama, Sierra Leone, Tanzania, and Venezuela.

On the first Sunday of 1985 we began two worship services. The first service was from 8:00 to 9:00 a.m., and the second was from 10:30 to 11:30 a.m. A number of choir members sang in both. The two services enabled us to reach more people.

In 1985 Veta and I planned to take a group to Israel, Egypt, and other places when terrorists captured the ship the *Achille Lauro*. The terrorists threw a wheelchair-bound Jewish-American passenger overboard and held other passengers hostage. We received a number of calls from members of our group hesitant to go abroad. I called our travel agent, who suggested we take the group to Scandinavia—Sweden, Denmark, and Norway—instead. The trip ended up being one of our most enjoyable ever. We took in the sights and sounds of those three countries and came home delighted, with a new appreciation for another part of Europe.

We finished the year giving over $25,000 to the Home Mission offering and $122,000 to the Lottie Moon offering. We overgave our church budget for the seventeenth year in a row. We adopted a $1,360,000 budget for 1986. I do not write these figures in vanity. I write them in gratitude to God and our church members. Each year we used the budget overage to underwrite folks on short-term mission assignments. In 1985 thirty-nine members served in eleven foreign countries—Australia, Chile, Denmark, Dominican Republic, England, Jamaica, Mali, Nigeria, Scotland, Sierra Leone, and South Korea.

Woodmont's forty-fifth anniversary occurred in 1986. We invited Dr. West to preach. We had an enjoyable time reminiscing and seeing church folk from yesteryear.

A Chinese church began meeting in our chapel at the same time we were worshipping in the meetinghouse each Sunday. Peter Kung, a member of Woodmont, pastored the church. Following morning worship, they gathered in the chapel for a Sunday dinner.

In July, our family drove to Fort Worth to paint my grandmother's house. My grandfather, Dad Brannon, had been dead for several years, and Bamaw now lived alone in a small frame house in the Tate Springs community, eight miles southeast of Fort Worth. Her house badly needed some sprucing up. Cecil was the pastor at Broadway Baptist in Fort Worth at the time, and he was able to help as well. We had to cut back the trees and shrubs from the house before we could do the painting. Donny was also helping. Bamaw watched from the front porch. She noticed our Chevrolet station wagon was larger than Cecil's car and said, "Billy Don, doesn't Cecil pastor a church larger than your church?" I replied, "Yes, he does." She then said, "Then why doesn't he drive a larger car than you do?" (Just so happened that Cecil's car was a Mercedes.) Donny walked over to her and said, "Bamaw, do you realize Uncle Cecil's car cost twice as much as Daddy's car?" She was shocked. She shook her head and said, "Well, all I've got to say is he didn't get much for his money." We all died laughing.

In 1986 we had sixty-three members serving in fifteen countries abroad. If this sounds like a broken record each year, it is a daggone good broken record. I continually reminded our people not to take mission involvement for granted. Hearing from so many whose lives had been changed from serving in overseas missions was refreshing. From their stories, sometimes we could not tell who had received the greatest benefit. Truth of the matter is everyone received a wonderful benefit.

Veta and I had the privilege of going to Warsaw, Poland, that year where I taught the Pauline epistles to the seminarians. The president of the Seminary was Gustav Ceisler. Our first Sunday there I preached at a church in Bialystok. We brought choir robes from Woodmont that we donated to the church. Over the next two weeks we spent our time teaching and visiting World War II sites. One afternoon we went to an apartment and visited with a lady who was part of the Warsaw Uprising in 1944. The Russian Army was five kilometers from Warsaw, so the Polish Underground fighters took to the streets. They drove the Germans out of the city thinking the Russians would come in and occupy; however, the Russians did not budge. The Germans counterattacked with tanks and infantry, and they recaptured the city. The fighting was fierce. The lady described all this in full that afternoon. We sat for almost two hours, spellbound. The Germans took her to a concentration camp where amazingly she survived. That afternoon is etched in my memory. We came home thanking God that we were born in the United States. Freedom is not something to be taken for granted.

We added a new ministry in 1987—the Pow Wow Club—for retired senior men. As pastor the only relationship I had with these men was when I visited them in the hospital. That was not very upbeat! I wanted to find a way to spend more time with them apart from the hospital or the funeral home. We met once a month to eat and just "powwow." The club was a great success. Everyone had a story and a joke to share. I always asked our staff to come. A few dragged their feet, but I told them, "Look, these are the people who pay our salary. They deserve our time and goodwill." And the staff graciously attended.

12

WOODMONT—TRAGEDIES AND MIRACLES

1988–1992

The year 1988 marked the WMU's centennial in Baptist life. The Woman's Missionary Union has meant so much to mission awareness, mission giving, and mission going; and our WMU ladies led the charge in having a celebration at our church. The day was both informational and inspirational.

Along the line of women's leadership, our deacons discussed changing our bylaws to enable women to serve as deacons. There were varied opinions, but fortunately, the discussion stayed between the fences. When all was said and done, a motion to present an amendment to the bylaws passed. The amendment stated that in the next deacon election in fall 1988, Woodmont would include women on the ballot. The deacons chose Bobbie Dunn as our first female deacon. Jenny Roberts would follow as our second female deacon.

Our Sunday School attendance was near 1,100, and we needed more education space. The church set in motion plans for a new preschool building that would come to fruition the following year. In May our church purchased the house directly behind our meetinghouse for a third missionary home.

During that summer Veta and I spent three weeks in different parts of Asia. I led a mission meeting in Thailand for a week, which was a refreshing experience. Some forty missionaries gathered at Pattaya and spent the days in Bible study, worship, and sharing. Next, we went to Bangkok for two days, to Singapore for a night, and then to Penang in Malaysia. For two weeks I taught the Pauline epistles at Malaysia Baptist Theological Seminary.

Amos Lee, a Southern Baptist Seminary graduate, was president of the seminary. There were about fifty students in attendance who were eager to learn. Most spoke English quite well. We stayed in a screened-in room on the second floor above the dining hall. In the mornings the monkeys awakened us, playing in the trees all around us. We all ate together in a dining hall where workers served two kinds of rice—wet and dry. The students' favorite menu, however, was fish heads and rice. That was more challenging than my stomach could take. The dining hall really needed fixing up, so I asked Amos if it would be all right if I painted the place. He was overjoyed. Veta said she would be glad to make curtains for the windows if they would get her the materials. We worked during the afternoons. Dr. Lee said that Malaysians who have college degrees do not do manual labor as they consider the work beneath them. Of course, I did not know that. This explained why so many students came by and said, "Dr. Sherman, have you ever done this before?" I would smile and reply, "All my life." They would look at me, shrug their shoulders, and walk on. We flew home with many good memories.

A major issue arose in Nashville in 1987 and again in 1988 when the gambling industry sought a foothold in Tennessee. Kentucky had pari-mutuel gambling on horse racing with the Kentucky Derby and other tracks. I did not feel that gambling was moral and, moreover, felt that many people would be abused by legalized gambling. Consequently, I called two of the highest profile clergymen in our city—Rubel Shelly and Steve Flatt. Steve was pastor of Madison Church of Christ, and Rubel was pastor of Woodmont Hills Church of Christ. Together we formed a coalition of churches to defeat the issue, with other denominations participating as well. We had meetings, made contacts, and conducted interviews with the three television stations. The campaign went on for several months. Feelings were strong on both sides of the issue. On election day voters defeated horse-track gambling. The governor, Ned McWherter, said in *The Tennessean*, "Dr. Bill Sherman is the conscience of Middle Tennessee."

The largest group of Woodmont members to participate in overseas missions occurred in 1988 with 112 members serving in ten countries. Incidentally, if anyone wants to know who went where, the information is available in *From This Corner: A History of Woodmont Baptist Church 1941–2017*, written by Susan Richardson. In addition to those who served overseas, eighty-two of our members served in six states at home. To look at these numbers in reflection is astounding.

Two things happened in 1988 that were deeply discouraging. First, we had a youth director leave his wife and two children and move to Texas with a deacon's wife. The story unfolded as I was waiting on him to join me on a visit to a family who had recently visited our church. He walked in wearing shorts and flip-flops. He informed me that they were leaving for Texas the next day. I was shocked. I said, "I'm not buying this. You have until tomorrow morning to rethink this and get your head screwed on right. I'll meet you here at 8:00 a.m." He nodded and walked out. The next morning, I had the chairman of the deacons and the chairman of the personnel committee sitting in my office with me when he walked in. I said, "Have you changed your mind?" He replied, "No, we are leaving town at 9:00 a.m." Both chairmen unloaded on him for the next twenty minutes. He merely shrugged his shoulders and walked out. We called a meeting of our youth and their parents for Saturday night in the choir room. We wanted them to know exactly what had transpired before the rumor mill cranked out all kinds of false stories. Concerned members packed the choir room. We told our young people the truth. We also wanted to discuss how we could minister to the deacon husband who was brokenhearted over the turn of events. Both the youth parents and the young people rallied support for the broken families left behind and the youth ministry going forward.

The other event that bruised us was that our music minister was getting a divorce and wanted to remain in his position. The deacons and the congregation were divided as to what to do. He was well-liked and was doing a good job with the music program. The discussion amongst the deacons went back and forth with one group saying that we needed to forgive and support him and the other group saying that we needed to teach our kids to be faithful in marriage by hiring a new leader who was a better example. We took a vote, and the forgiveness folk prevailed by a razor-thin majority. Part of the negativity also came from the fact that a few years earlier this minister had a drinking problem. Our church quietly underwrote his recovery at the Vanderbilt Institute for the Treatment of Addiction. The music folk were pleased with the deacons' vote. Others in the congregation were not pleased. We moved on.

On top of all this that was going on at church, we had a family emergency at home. I returned from a revival that I was leading one night, and Veta met me at the door. She said, "Honey, we have some bad news. The report came back about the mole on Donny's back. It is melanoma." Donny was thirty-one years old. I had buried Franz Claypool, who died from metastatic melanoma, two years earlier. In just a few days we were at MD Anderson Cancer Center in Houston for treatment. Doctors there performed a wide excision on Donny's back. To err on the side of caution, doctors later performed another operation that took the lymph system from under his right arm. I hoped we would never have to return to that place again, but only the future would tell. The church folk were wonderful in their support.

Two other events took place in 1988 with my parents. First, Mother broke her hip. Fortunately, Cecil was pastoring in Fort Worth and could take care of things. Veta and I made our way there for Mother's surgery, which went well. We had a good visit. Dad also had two minor strokes. As we left the nursing home, I told Veta I believed this would be the last time we would see Dad this side of the Jordan. She said, "Honey, he is as tough as a boot. He'll bounce back." I said, "Maybe so." As we said our goodbyes and walked up the hall, I turned and looked back. Dad was leaning on the door jamb. He waved and said, "Son, I'll be a-seein' ya." Those were the last words I ever heard my daddy say. He died in November at the age of eighty-seven. Mother and Daddy were married for sixty-two years. His service was the day after Thanksgiving in Fort

Worth. I could not have asked for a finer father. He was born on November 11, 1901, in Hartsville, Tennessee, the son of a Baptist preacher. He grew up in seventeen different places in Tennessee, Oklahoma, and Texas as his daddy moved from church to church throughout his childhood. His last stop was in Fort Worth where he was forced to drop out of high school to work in a garage to support his mother and his siblings when his daddy died of a heart attack. It was in Fort Worth that he married my mother in 1926. They began their life in the house where I grew up. He was a gregarious, people person—a churchman through and through. He devoted his life to his family and his Lord. He probably has a group of junior boys and girls singing "Our Best" in glory as I write. I was blessed to have a Daddy like him.

Our twentieth anniversary at Woodmont was in 1989. The church graciously gave Veta and me a two-week trip to Korea and China. But for now, it was full speed ahead on our new preschool building. The total cost was $1,900,000. We had a major rally with a dinner at the Opryland Hotel, and the end result was our membership pledging $1,800,000! Construction began, and we completed the building in October.

Another positive thing happened this year. Our fellowship hall could not accommodate our Wednesday evening suppers anymore. We gathered a group of men, took the walls down from the

Present Woodmont Baptist facilities for worship and ministry.

Sunday School classes on the east side of the hall, which enlarged the room considerably, and spruced up the walls with paint, thus saving the church a good bit of money.

On Friday evenings we began a ministry for the Messianic Jews. About seventy-five believing Jews needed a place to worship. When I heard about the situation, I contacted their leader, who was overjoyed to come to Woodmont. Each week they arrived around 6:00 p.m., ate a light meal, and followed with a worship service. They sang Jewish songs, accompanied by guitars and dance—the men danced with the men, and the women danced with the women. They did not worry about time. It was serendipity! It was also inspirational. They asked me to preach their first service. The service began about 7:30 p.m., and I stood up to preach at 9:15 p.m. Veta wondered where in the world I had been when I walked in a little before 10:00 p.m. Our congregation was glad to provide places for the Chinese church and Messianic Jews to worship.

Summer came, and we were excited to take our anniversary trip to Asia along with a group of around twenty-five folks from the church. We flew to Seoul, South Korea, and visited the Governor's Palace. As we walked through the garden, we heard a group of boys and girls singing in Korean, "I've got the joy, joy, joy, joy down in my heart . . ." We walked over and visited with them. They were from a Presbyterian orphanage. Our next stop was Beijing where we worshipped in a non-denominational church. We then proceeded to Tiananmen Square. (Remember this was during the Chinese Uprising in 1989.) The students were there by the thousands. They were marching, chanting, and holding banners. Our Chinese guide was nervous and would not allow us to leave the bus. When the demonstrators saw that we were Americans, they cheered. We arrived home on a Monday, and the Chinese military killed the students the next Friday. We were so grateful to be home.

A smaller group of Woodmont members were involved in overseas missions in 1989. Forty-six members went to six countries, serving in construction, evangelism, and medical needs and sewing graduation gowns. Our youth went to Pennsylvania to do

Presentation to Keith Parks of the 1989 Lottie Moon Offering of over $151,000.

A large portion of short-term mission volunteers who fulfilled over 900 assignments in overseas volunteer mission work from 1977 to 1997.

Backyard Bible Clubs, and our singles went to a different location in Pennsylvania for a construction project.

On the home front, our youngest son, David, married Beverly Krantz in 1989, a lovely girl from Ashland City whom he met while working at Baptist Hospital. They would later give us three beautiful grandchildren: Eli, born July 31, 1997; Jesse, born July 19, 1999;

and Rachel, born April 13, 2001. Debbie, our daughter, finished her eye surgery residency in ophthalmology at Vanderbilt and completed a fellowship in eye plastic surgery at the University of Wisconsin, in Madison, Wisconsin. Donny was employed at the Southwestern Company in Nashville.

The first year that our Sunday School topped the 1,200 mark was in 1990. We were both thankful and pleased. Another high mark that year was that the church receipts—budget, mission offerings, and the building fund—totaled $1,604,228. We were truly blessed by the faithfulness of our folk in giving. Our singles built another Habitat for Humanity house this year as well.

April 1990 was a brutal week in the Sherman household. Donny, who was now thirty-two, had enjoyed nineteen months of good health after his initial diagnosis of melanoma. The oncologists had warned us from the get-go that his tumor carried a significant chance of returning or spreading within the first five years after the diagnosis. Unfortunately, Donny's tumor did spread.

One evening he had a severe headache that necessitated a trip to the emergency room. A CT scan showed an abnormal tumor in the left side of his brain in and around his speech center. Dr. Jim Hayes, an excellent neurosurgeon, performed Donny's brain surgery, removing most of the tumor. He stopped short of removing the tumor in the actual speech center as he did not want Donny to lose his ability to speak in what we thought would be his last months of life. Now that the tumor had spread to his brain, the odds were not good for his survival. Sadly, there were no treatments available that could give him much hope.

Several weeks later Donny woke up in the middle of the night with severe stomach pain. A tumor was causing a bowel obstruction. This condition required immediate, lifesaving surgery. Unfortunately, the surgery revealed the grim news that his tumor had spread to the lymph nodes.

Further imaging tests revealed that he also had a lesion on his lung indicating further tumor spread. This extensive spread of melanoma put him with a prognosis of less than three months to live. Furthermore, the doctors told us that all treatments available had a less than 5 percent response rate with less than a 5 percent survival rate. The future did not look encouraging. We all took a deep breath.

Prayers and support from friends, family, and members of churches all over the Southeast and Texas sustained us during this difficult time. Donny was firm in his faith and unwavering in his good attitude. He never asked, "Why me?" He took each day as it came and made the most of every opportunity in front of him. He showed amazing spunk.

Such a grave prognosis being laid at our family's feet was almost unfathomable. Donny had so many unrealized dreams, including having a family and doing so many more wonderful things in his life. The consensus recommendation from many well-trained physicians in Nashville was for us to go to a melanoma center for further treatment. We chose MD Anderson in Houston.

As Donny lay in the bed at Baptist Hospital recovering from abdominal surgery, a team of doctors planned his sequence of radiation first in Nashville and then at MD Anderson. Our daughter, Debbie, a second-year ophthalmology resident at Vanderbilt, caught up with Dr. Bill Johnston, a respected surgical oncologist, in the hallway outside Donny's room and asked him, "Dr. Johnston, would you ask my brother and his wife to consider saving sperm before he starts radiation and chemotherapy? If by some miracle he lives, this might allow them the option of in vitro fertilization and give them a chance of having a family." As if an angel tapped him, Dr. Johnston did not question or hesitate and said, "Yes, of course!" He went in to speak to Donny and his wife, Tena, and they began to make plans. Looking back now, it appears the angel must have also tapped and inspired Debbie to ask Dr. Johnston that simple question. In reality, it was not a logical question when the odds were so grim for survival. Time would tell if that decision to plan for a little one would come to fruition.

After Donny recovered from surgery, he was a groomsman in Debbie's wedding at the end of May. He then returned to Houston for many challenging months of chemotherapy. For the next eighteen months he was in various treatment protocols for his melanoma.

Debbie married Tim Siktberg, a young man from Indiana whom she met at church while attending medical school. I had the privilege of officiating their wedding at Woodmont. Tim grew up in a Christian home, and his family were faithful church members. He was a perfect match for her, and their personalities complemented each other. We were so pleased to welcome him into our family.

Donny finally finished his treatment after a solid year in Houston. Veta spent months by his side giving him loving care. We were overjoyed when he came back to good ole Nashville, Tennessee!

Then the day came for the wonderful miracle! On August 17, 1992, thanks to in vitro fertilization, Jordan Christena Sherman came to bless all of us, especially Donny and Tena. Two years had passed since Donny had courageously completed a year of experimental chemo and immune therapy. Amazingly, all his tumors had completely vanished, surprising even the oncology team at MD Anderson. Not a single other patient in his clinical trial survived. God gave Donny this special gift. And God further blessed him with twenty-five more precious years of life. We were thankful for God's gift of those years; however, we were indebted to the excellent care of the competent physicians and nurses at MD Anderson, especially Dr. Sewa Legha.

Jordan continues to carry on Donny's legacy of love for life, hard work, and a commitment to making a difference. She works as a CRNA (certified registered nurse anesthetist), helping patients every day. She is married to Jason, and they currently live in Springfield, Tennessee.

A bright spot in our lives this year was when Veta and I moved her parents to Nashville. We were able to move them into our neighborhood just two blocks away, and they quickly joined Woodmont. Dad and Mom Cole were like a second set of parents to me. Dad was a super carpenter; in fact, he could do any kind of work—electrical, plumbing, you name it.

We had fifty-seven people serve in seven countries this year. Although the number varied from year to year, the good work that they did was constant.

The fundamentalists completed their takeover of the SBC boards and agencies at the Southern Baptist Convention in New Orleans in 1990. Many Baptists were apprehensive about what would happen to our mission endeavors and our seminaries. The moderate pastors announced a meeting in Atlanta, Georgia, on August 23. We had hoped for two hundred people—3,100 came. This was the beginning of the Cooperative Baptist Fellowship (CBF), which came into being to perpetuate Baptist ideals—priesthood of the believer, soul liberty, congregational authority in our churches, and the pastor as servant leader rather than ruler of the church.

In 1991 our Sunday School reached the 1,300 mark. Singles were clipping along at two hundred each Sunday. The telephone ministry for our television service fielded 678 calls for the year. We were meeting our budget. Things were sailing along well. 1991 was also Woodmont's fiftieth anniversary.

An issue that came up later in the year concerned budget planning. The Foreign Mission Board founded the Theological Seminary in Rüschlikon, Switzerland, in 1949 to educate European Baptist preachers for Christian ministry. The fundamentalists running the SBC planned to defund Rüschlikon for their beliefs about the role of women in the church. I shared the situation with our people and asked if we could assist in the funding to support our European Baptists. Some of our members, who were loyalists to the SBC, were not pleased. The fundamentalists fired Al Shackleford, the head of Baptist Press, Russell Dilday, the president of Southwestern Baptist Seminary, and Lloyd Elder, the president of the Baptist Sunday School Board. Were these men immoral or inefficient? No. The fundamentalists wanted to put like-minded men in the positions to perpetuate their narrow, fundamentalist views. This situation was a tragedy and the beginning of a sharp decline in the Southern Baptist Convention. Unfortunately, the average layman in the pew did not know what was happening to the convention. I felt the strong need to inform our people in order that we maintain true Baptist principles.

In 1991, mother died. She grew up on a farm eight miles from the Poly neighborhood. She met Daddy at Poly Baptist. She was of Puritan stock; her life focused on the church. A WMU (Woman's Missionary Union) circle met monthly at our house. Never, ever did we have the conversation, "Shall we go to church today?" That was a given. All us kids had chores around the house. She kept us between the fences, but she loved us to death. She died on Christmas Day. Both my beloved parents are buried in Mount Olivet Cemetery in Fort Worth. Actually, they are not buried there; what is buried there are the bodies in which they used to live. Thankfully, they are very much alive with the Lord!

13
WOODMONT—BATTLES ON THE INSIDE

1993–1997

In 1993 I had served Woodmont as pastor for twenty-five years. The congregation always treated us well, and the twenty-fifth anniversary was no exception. The church held a celebratory afternoon service on January 31. Governor Ned McWherter sent congratulatory words, and Mayor Phil Bredesen read a proclamation. The church unveiled a portrait of Veta and me, named the new preschool building the Bill & Veta Sherman Children's Building, and gave us a generous retirement annuity. The folk were remarkably kind.

The church listed a number of highlights on the back of the anniversary service program. Over 4,700 new members had joined the congregation, 961 by baptism. Church membership and Sunday School attendance had more than doubled. Over one hundred fifty thousand viewers worshipped by television each Sunday. Woodmont members had filled 794 overseas mission assignments in thirty-eight countries, and support for mission causes had increased tenfold. Mission activities included a Chinese congregation and a Messianic Jewish congregation, which met weekly at the church. For twenty-two years we had held interracial worship services with Fifteenth Avenue Baptist Church. Church members had built three houses with Habitat for Humanity. When I read these statements, I was eternally grateful for what our folk had done for the Kingdom. Serving these people as pastor was a joy.

Shortly after the anniversary service, one of our laymen who did a monthly audit of all written checks informed me that a staff member had purchased items costing thousands of dollars without church approval. This was clearly not within church guidelines. I thanked him and told him I would address the problem. I walked across the building and talked with the staff member. He was long-standing in his position and well-liked; however, there had been other issues as well. He was an alcoholic, now sober, for which the church forgave him and paid his rehabilitation. His marriage dissolved. All this added up. He had quite a following in the church, and I sought to work things out privately with him. We preached to Nashville every Sunday on television, and I did not want anyone in a leadership position at Woodmont to compromise the truths of the gospel. We had a long conversation during which he was very defensive, saying we needed to let the issue drop. I insisted that, as ministers, we must take a course of integrity. We made no progress toward a resolution, and I left.

I realized shortly afterwards that I had made a mistake—I should have had a third party in the room when we met. Within days, two very different versions of our meeting came out—his and mine. The next Sunday afternoon a group gathered in a Green Hills apartment clubhouse to hear his version of our meeting. Afterward, I began to receive phone calls, including one from the chairman of the deacons who was active in this man's ministry. His people came on strong and told me that I must apologize. For several weeks various groups held meetings about the matter. I talked to four of the most trusted men in our church who were surprised and disappointed by the attitudes of this man's followers. They, too, had tried to talk with some of these folks without success. A month went by, and this minister finally resigned. Afterward, the air needed to be cleared. My leadership remained in question. I wanted to do the right thing for the church, so I wrote an open letter to our church members. I shared that some among the membership felt the time had come for me to move on and that I would do whatever the membership felt was right. I stated that in two weeks, following the morning worship, the church family could affirm the future of the pulpit with a standing vote without discussion.

On May 16 we had our largest Sunday School attendance ever with over 1,300 members present. The front page of *The Tennessean* ran a small article. All three televisions stations were present, and I told the reporters that they must stay in the foyers as this was a worship service. My father-in-law was in the senior men's class that day. The teacher asked Ted Register to lead the opening prayer. The men bowed their heads, and Ted said, "Lord, thank you for this day. Be with our church today; and Lord, we pray that all folks who don't support our pastor will get the hell out of here." All the men were shocked! When they opened their eyes, a loud burst of laughter filled the room. However, the situation was not a laughing matter. I was disappointed that it had come to a confrontation. A number of our deacons had talked with these folks, but their minds were made up. Several had talked to me. They said, "Preacher, you are the problem." I told them I certainly had made mistakes along the way; however, the mistakes were of the head and not the heart. I also told them that church leaders MUST lead moral lives. This had been the breakdown. There is no substitute for moral character in leadership! Were they saying that staff members should not be examples?

We placed chairs in the aisles to accommodate the large crowds. I preached on Jesus' words regarding Peter's confession, "Thou art the Christ, the Son of the living God" (Matt 16:16 KJV). A church is a group of believers who proclaim Christ is the Son of the living God. I preached with a heavy heart. I realized that church leaders can only be useful if they live the faith they affirm. I was not looking for a fight, but I was not willing to look the other way when something less than moral was a pattern for a staff member. The service ended. I shared that we would now have the church act as to present and future pastoral leadership. At this time a young adult deacon walked up on the platform. I did not know what he had in mind. I looked straight ahead and anchored my position in front of the pulpit. He leaned in and said, "I am not in favor of this action. If you feel as I do, walk out with me." He turned and walked off the platform along with a dozen other people. I asked four of the finest laymen to make the call as to the vote. Marvin Sharpton, Arliss Roaden, DeVaughn Woods, and Arthur Piepmeir each observed the vote in the three downstairs sections and the balcony. I said, "All those who feel that our present pastor should continue as pastor, please stand." Virtually the whole congregation stood—downstairs and upstairs. They looked around and began to cheer. This went on for about ten seconds. I asked the membership to be seated. The four deacons approached me and said, "Pastor, we don't need to have another vote as the first one was overwhelming." I told them that I had promised the membership that they would have that privilege, so I told the congregation what the deacons had said. I then asked, "Is there anyone who would like to continue with the process?" No one raised a hand. I said, "Our deliberation is concluded." Applause broke out again. We stood and sang our benediction, and I went to the back door as always. I stood for almost an hour as folks came by and shared kind words. I was aware that the whole ordeal had been a bruising experience for our church family, and I regretted the whole situation. But as I searched my heart, I determined that we must be loyal to our Christian values and dedicated to our biblical principles.

The rest of 1993 was a time of healing and adjustment. Some members felt led to unite with other churches; as a result, we moved to one morning worship service, and Sunday School attendance was adjusted to eight hundred.

An unusual occurrence happened during this time. Cora and Nora Burns, members of Grandview Baptist Church, informed us that they had willed their house and property to Woodmont. I called the ladies and went and visited with them. They said to me, "Come in, Dr. Sherman, you are no stranger here. You have come into this house every Sunday for the last seventeen years." They shared that our worship service, by means of the television ministry, was a blessing in their home. We had a good visit and stayed in touch. Within the next three years I led each of their memorial services. The appraisal district valued their house and property at $357,000.

Our overseas mission ministry had fourteen members serving in seven different countries. In addition, our youth conducted VBS in two different states. Our world mission offering goal was $90,000; we gave $96,000. By the end of 1993 Woodmont had filled 814 overseas short-term mission assignments.

On the home front, Debbie, now an eye plastic surgeon, had conducted groundbreaking research in orbital lymphatics in primates during her Ophthalmic Plastic Surgery Fellowship at the University of Wisconsin. She received an award recognizing her significant contribution to her field in 1992 and was asked to present the paper to the European Society of Ophthalmic Plastic Surgery in Nice, France, in 1993. Veta and I wanted to be there for her special recognition, so we flew to France. Afterward, we rented a car and drove across the country, visiting Lyon, the Loire Valley, Avignon, Cluny, the Normandy Battlefield, Château-Thierry and Belleau Wood of World War I fame, Versailles, and Paris. Of course, we did not speak French. One day when we stopped in the boonies, I pointed to a picture on the menu that I thought was steak with *pommes frites* or French fries. The waiter shrugged his shoulders and brought me liver and French fries. We all laughed. We arrived safely back home after another great trip.

In 1994 our church body was still healing and adjusting; however, a good spirit was in the family. Our membership was not what it had been, yet we were seeking to be what God would have us to be. A highlight in the early part of the year was paying off our debt. We retired the preschool building debt from the money we received from Cora and Nora Burns' wills. When Easter came, we had a joint worship service with our neighbor churches—Woodmont Christian, Calvary Methodist, Trinity Presbyterian, and Woodmont Hills Church of Christ. The church choir was growing, reaching the fifty mark in the fall. Our Home Mission offering goal was $20,000. The church gave just under $19,000. Our world mission offering goal was $90,000, combining monies to both the Lottie Moon offering for the Southern Baptists and the World Mission offering for the Cooperative Baptist Fellowship. Thankfully, we met the goal.

In October 1994 Veta and I flew to Russia with a gift of $30,000 for the Russian Baptist Congress in Moscow from the Cooperative Baptist Fellowship. Cecil, my brother, was director of the CBF at the time. The Baptist Congress was composed of Baptist churches throughout the former Soviet Union. Over 1,700 Russian Baptists, mostly men, were in attendance. We presented the money to the leaders, who were most appreciative. They would use the money to begin new churches up and down the Ob River Valley. The participants were unapologetically evangelistic, and we were impressed with their zeal. On the last night of the gathering, there was a time of prayer. Throughout the hall you could hear men weeping. At the close of the meeting, I discussed the scene with a gentleman from northwestern Africa who had beamed the gospel into Russia for years. He shared that the Russians present were thankful because this was the first meeting in memory in which members of the NKVD (Russian Secret Police) were not present to place attendees in prison. I came away with great admiration for those brave Russian Baptists. I also had a greater gratitude for the privilege of living in the United States.

Debbie and Tim became parents with the arrival of Jonathan in 1994, followed by Jackson in 1997, giving us two wonderful grandsons. Debbie received a nice feather in her cap when the American Society of Ophthalmic Plastic and Reconstructive Surgeons presented her with their annual award for outstanding contribution to the field, the second woman to receive the award. We were quite proud. Donny continued his cancer treatment. David, our youngest, finished his LPN degree in nursing, and Baptist Hospital in Nashville employed him right afterwards. It has been a blessing to have children who are a doctor and a nurse. They have cared for their parents in a wonderful way.

Woodmont ended the year overgiving our budget by $32,000 and overgiving our mission offering as well. Abingdon Press invited me to be a consulting editor for The New Interpreter's Bible Commentary. I was honored and gladly consented. My assignment was to give observations from a pastoral perspective. The work was enjoyable. Abingdon published the commentary in 1998. Our members did short-term mission-ary work in two cities in Chile and two cities in Venezuela in 1994. Our youth group painted a church and led Backyard Bible Clubs in Manchester, Tennessee.

Early in 1995 Joanne James, my secretary, retired after serv-ing twenty-seven years. After all that time she and her husband, Ed, were like family. They were faithful members of Judson Bap-tist Church, where Ed was a deacon and Joanne was the director of an adult Sunday School department. Working together had been a joy, and I appreciated all that she had done.

A new ministry that we began in 1995 was the Alcoholics Anonymous ministry led by our youngest son, David. He was a perfect fit for this ministry as he is a great people person. We hoped to minister to people with an alcohol problem who needed this service and to give them a second chance. A new beginning is what the gospel is all about.

We once again enjoyed our joint worship service with Fif-teenth Avenue, our African American Baptist friends. Rev. Enoch Jones retired, and Rev. William Simmons was their new shepherd.

Veta and I led a group to the Holy Land in the summer. A highlight of the trip was observing the Lord's Supper in a garden beneath Golgotha. We gazed at the tomb down the way and Skull Hill to our right while the public address system played "In the Garden." As we reflected upon what happened in this place two thousand years ago, we were deeply moved. If you go to the Holy Land with faith, you return home with faith; if you go with doubt, you return home with doubt. These trips through the years were both enjoyable and inspirational. We were so fortunate to have been able to take them.

That fall a group of city leaders, both black and white, approached me and asked me to run for mayor. The present mayor had gone all out to bring professional football to Nash-ville at a considerable cost to the city's budget. The Houston Oil-ers were out of sorts with their agreement with the town fathers. In some ways I would have liked to run. The African American community strongly urged me to do so. However, I did not feel that politics was my calling. I thanked them and remained pastor of Woodmont.

One afternoon in late summer when I came in from playing tennis, I noticed a bump with a small, black core in the center on my leg between my knee and ankle. Debbie happened to come by the house, and I asked her what the bump might be. She looked and replied, "Dad, I don't know, but you had better go see a doctor." I said, "Deb, you are several cuts above a witch doctor. What is this?" Within an hour she had an appointment for me the next day with a dermatologist. The doctor deadened the spot, cut a slug from my leg, and sent the sample to the lab. The following day we drove to Fort Worth for the CBF meeting. A few days later Debbie called and said, "Dad, you have a melanoma. Please come home as soon as you can." I took a deep breath and wondered what the future held.

When I arrived home, surgery was awaiting. The doctor wanted to take a wide excision to get all the cancer cells. Cecil's daughter, Genie, was married to a radiologist. They lived in Madison, Wisconsin. Her husband, Doug, called and said, "Uncle Bill, if you can come to Madison, I can give you a PET scan without charge." He had a government grant and needed more patients. I was eligible. So, Tim, Debbie, Veta, and I flew to Madison. The scan lasted all day. We then went to MD Anderson in Houston where Dr. Legha, Donny's doctor, took me as a patient. He mapped a protocol, and we returned home for the wide excision at Vanderbilt Hospital. The doctor found no additional cancer cells and told me that I had a fifty-fifty chance that the cancer would not return. We moved on, hoping such would be the case. The church members were so gracious. I missed four Sundays from the pulpit.

In January 1996 we received the good news that we had over-given our 1995 budget with a final figure of $1,198,000. The folk were good stewards. In the spring our folk built a fourth Habitat for Humanity house. These projects were always hard work, but enjoyable. I appreciated getting to know the recipients of the houses. Each was so grateful and thrilled in every case. The

Habitat program requires a new homeowner to have worked on houses for others before he is eligible for his own home. When his turn comes, he must also work on his own house. I appreciated the ministry that the Habitat folk provided.

Come summer the Performing Arts Center in Nashville announced their schedule for the year. One of the musicals was *Oh! Calcutta!*, which I had never heard of. A few weeks before it came to town, a long article appeared in the morning paper describing the upcoming performance. Most of the cast would be nude throughout. The songs were crude and lewd. The Center would only allow folks over eighteen in the door. This was to occur in our city's Performing Arts Center? To me, allowing this production implied the blessings of the city upon such trash. If a cast performed the musical in a privately-owned strip club, that would be a different matter. The tax monies of New Testament Christians in Nashville underwrote the Performing Arts Center. I was incensed. That musical was endorsing and advocating everything that the New Testament condemned. On Sunday morning I preached on "Wholesome Christian Sexuality." The text came from Paul's admonition to Timothy. He wrote, ". . . keep thyself pure" (1 Tim 5:22 KJV). There were plenty of courtesans walking around Ephesus. One could indulge in union in those days with the blessings of a pagan society. I felt that our city needed to hear the message affirming what is right and wrong in sex, and our television ministry provided that opportunity. In the introduction to the message, I challenged what the other side of the aisle always says—for mature adults. I pointed out that mature adults live a disciplined life by keeping sexual relations within the boundaries of marriage. The sign on the door for the performance should read, "for immature adults." These are the adults who live by their glands. I shared a common analogy. I grow a garden each year because Veta and I enjoy homegrown tomatoes. I plant the tomato plants in soil; however, if I dump a shovelful of soil onto our living room carpet, the soil becomes dirt. Sexual expression can either be moral or immoral. Wholesome sexual relations belong within the bounds of marriage. When so expressed, there is no guilt. In any other situation, problems will ensue. The congregation sat mesmerized. As I stood at the door after the sermon, person after person affirmed the message. Sunday afternoon the phone rang constantly, and the phone continued to ring at church all day Monday. Letters by the score came to the church the next week. On Monday afternoon I went home and picked up the evening paper, the *Nashville Banner*. The headlines read, "No Calcutta!" with a picture of our service on the front page. Of all the sermons I had preached in Nashville over the past twenty-nine years, this one received the greatest response. I was shocked. Ninety percent of the people appreciated my stand while 10 percent labeled me as a bigoted, narrow-minded Baptist preacher.

In the fall my cancer reappeared as a nodule on my shin. The cancer required not only surgery and chemotherapy but a skin graft as well. The surgeon at Vanderbilt Hospital had to cut the muscle and roll it onto my shin for protection. The graft was a real challenge. Six rounds of chemo treatments followed. I was out of circulation for about three months. Cancer was a challenge like none I had ever faced. The church folk were gracious, and I appreciated their support. I hoped that I was getting ahead of melanoma. My heart went out to Veta. She had a husband and son in cancer treatment at the same time. I found that faith, family, and friends were the finest support for folks in our situation.

We had seventeen mission folks who went to seven different countries in 1996. Veta and I were in this group. Six of us went to Prague in Czechoslovakia. We worked to prepare a facility to accommodate the International Baptist Theological Seminary (IBTS), which was moving from Switzerland to Prague due to the high cost of living in Switzerland. We appreciated the ministry of the IBTS.

As 1997 unfolded I realized that it would be in the best interest of the church for me to retire. I was sixty-five years old and in my thirtieth year as pastor. The cancer was casting a fog over my future as well as my ministry. Woodmont had always been there for me. We had walked the trail together through good times and tough times. Thankfully, the ups had outnumbered the downs. I shared my feelings with the deacons and staff, and we laid the groundwork for the transition. First, the church called Pete Ford, a retired Baptist preacher, as interim pastor. Pete had served at Eastland Baptist Church in Nashville for over twenty years. If, over the course of the next year, cancer put me out of commission, Pete would be in place.

Another plus came in April when Richard Dickerson came as our new minister of music. He and his family moved to Nashville from First Baptist Church, Union City, Tennessee. He hit the ground running, and the choir almost doubled in the first month. He resurrected the handbell choir. Richard was a great people person, brimming with enthusiasm. He was also a team player.

In the summer the church formed an interim pastor search committee so that when I stepped out of the picture on the last Sunday in December, the new interim would be in place. Ironically, the chairman of this committee was Carlton Carter, the church member who had recommended me to the Woodmont pulpit committee in 1967. He asked me to come to their first meeting. I told the committee that Baptist life had changed in the last ten years. For example, historically Baptists have had the congregation make major decisions. Many pastors now feel that *they* are the ruler of the church. I encouraged them to find a pastor who honors Baptist beliefs and polity—a true, historic Baptist. I never met with them again.

I only needed to cover one more base before I retired—a celebration committee. The church acted and chose Jack Robinson Jr. as chairman. Jack approached Veta and me and said the church wanted to do something special; however, they would like for us to have some input. We thanked him and said, "If the church plans to sell the parsonage, could we have first refusal? We would love to stay in our home." He replied, "I think that is a great idea." In a November business meeting Jack presented the idea. Everyone was for it, except how would the price be determined? Everybody had a different price in mind. Many simply wanted to give us the residence. One of our young adults had a creative idea. He said, "Let's give everyone here a card. Write on the card what you feel the price should be—full market value or nothing. We will add up the prices and divide the total by the number of cards. Then the church members will have truly decided what the price should be." The members did as suggested. When the smoke cleared, the price of the parsonage was $81,000. Veta and I were touched and most grateful.

A wonderful number of church members served in voluntary missions around the world in 1997. Forty-one members served in eight different countries. Twenty-two members served in Poland while twelve went to Venezuela. Other nations served were Zimbabwe, South Africa, Guatemala, Chile, Costa Rica, and France. When you add up all the overseas mission assignments filled by Woodmont members through the years, the total is over 927. Did 927 different people go? No. About 348 volunteers went time after time. Veta and I had the joy of serving in Jamaica, Poland, Russia, the Czech Republic, Guatemala, Brazil, Thailand, West Malaysia, and Hong Kong. With this many folks going year after year, it is no surprise that our church's world mission offering was over $100,000 year after year. In fact, one year it was over $156,000. Veta and I are proud as punch of the mission actions of our church members through the years.

The church set our parting celebration for November 16 to avoid the rush of Thanksgiving and Christmas. After the worship service we had a lovely luncheon in Fellowship Hall. At 1:30 p.m. everyone gathered in the meetinghouse. Dr. Arliss Roaden gave introductory remarks. Senator Doug Henry; Dr. Allen West; Councilman Charles French; Dr. Albert Berry, member of Fifteenth Avenue Baptist Church; and Dr. James Porch, executive director of the Tennessee Baptist Convention, each gave special greetings. Others speaking that day were folks that had been associated with us from earlier days—Dr. Bob Feather, vice president of Baylor University; Harold Phillips; Dr. Cecil Sherman; Kathleen Horrell; and DeVaughn Woods. Many stories and much laughter were shared by the kind remarks of the special guests. Veta received some beautiful earrings, and I got a John Deere riding mower. A surprise gift was one of the pulpit chairs from the chapel, which David had repaired and refinished. The celebration was an hour and a half of reflections, thankfulness, and hearing from old friends. What a "wonderful day in the neighborhood."

Our last Sunday was December 28, 1997. The meetinghouse was full. Many folks came from other churches. I said a farewell to our television congregation during the offering time just as I had always visited with them each Sunday. Although this was a hard time for me, it was a good time. Ninety percent of the people present had joined during the thirty years of my pastorate. As pastor, church members become family. I had preached as best I could through the years. I shared that a wonderful, loving, and powerful God was going to take care of Woodmont Baptist Church. I placed the congregation in His hands. I thanked the members for their wonderful love and support through the years. Standing at the back door following the service was as hard as the sermon had been. I have never hugged so many people in all my life. We drove home with a ton of memories. My time at Woodmont was a great run. I thought of the inscription I read long ago on the walls of a football stadium: And There Shall Be No Regrets! In the main, those were my feelings. When we got home, I gave Veta a great, big hug. We thanked God for it all and started thinking about our future. I looked out and saw my new John Deere tractor and broke into a smile.

14
PLAYING TAG WITH CANCER

1998–2003

Heaven knows that many folks have had battles with cancer. I am by no means an authority on the subject. I simply want to share what happened to me. My initial encounter with melanoma, as previously mentioned, was in 1995 with a wide excision operation. It reappeared in 1996 and 1997, each time necessitating operations and skin grafts. I was on a protocol of alpha interferon to stimulate my immune system to fight the cancer until April 1998, when I became allergic to the drug, and the treatment ceased.

Eventually, doctors discovered small nodules on the back of my thigh between the knee and hip. They were malignant. Our daughter, Debbie, injected interferon in them every other night for six months. Again, in a routine scan in 2000, doctors discovered a malignant tumor in the groin of my right leg. Dr. Ramsdell, a surgeon, removed it at St. Luke's Hospital in Houston. This occurrence demanded chemotherapy over a period of several months. Friends in Houston were immensely kind during this period. Ironically, John and Joan Scales, whom we had served with as students in Stillwater, Oklahoma, in the 1960s, graciously allowed us to live with them during the months of chemo treatments. John had been the Baptist Student Union director at Oklahoma State in those years. I began chemo feeling like a U.S. Marine—I was not going to let cancer put me on the mat! But I can tell you, you do not handle cancer; it handles you! I began each round of chemo in the hospital on Sunday. The chemo entered my veins for seven days and nights. Then I stayed twenty-four more hours for observation. When my oncologist, Dr. Legha, walked into my room I would say, "Doc, why do you keep me here for twenty-four hours of observation—to see if I'm going to kick the bucket?" His smile turned sober, and he nodded his head up and down. After six months we finally returned to Nashville.

The next step in my pursuit to overcome melanoma took place at the University of Virginia Medical School in Charlottesville, Virginia, in 2001. Dr. Slingluff was leading an experiment to find a vaccine for melanoma. Dr. Legha explained to us that the trials were in the early stages of development; however, if we wanted to pursue the vaccine, there was no harm. I applied and was accepted. That fall we drove to Charlottesville every Monday for eleven weeks. After each treatment we drove back to Richmond to spend the night with my brother, Cecil. After a brief visit we drove back to Nashville on Wednesday. The fall leaves between Nashville and Charlottesville were spectacular that year. The trip was a bit arduous but would be well worth the trouble if it took care of the cancer.

My cancer treatment and prognosis were going well until spring 2003. On a Saturday morning I awoke to severe abdominal pain. I could not even get out of bed. We called Debbie. I ended up in the emergency room at St. Thomas Hospital. I had never experienced that kind of pain with any injury or surgery. Dr. Hargreaves came into the room and said, "Dr. Sherman, with your medical history it is not appropriate to do any tests. We must simply go in there and find out what the problem is." He added, "I do this surgery on a weekly basis, and we might find that you have a number of precancerous nodes up and down your digestive tract. I just want to prepare you for what may be the case." I gave him the green light to do what he had to do. The situation did not look encouraging.

When I opened my eyes in recovery, David, our youngest son, was sitting by the bed. He looked at me with a grin bigger than a Chessy cat. He exclaimed, "Dad, we have some great news!" I replied, "Well, lay it on me. I could stand some good news right now." He stood up, and his voice got louder as he said, "No tumor! No nodes! The good news is that there was not a tumor that needs further chemo or immune therapy! Your stomach incision is from your sternum to Beersheba. Attendants in the operating room took out all your intestinal tract and felt for nodules. Then they put it back. It will take several days for the tract to get back in place." I asked him what had caused the pain. He said that I had a bowel obstruction in my ileum, the organ that connects the large and small intestines. Frankly, I did not even know I had an ileum. The bowel obstruction had destroyed the wall of my intestine, and bodily fluids had poured into my abdomen. Peritonitis had set in, causing my severe abdominal pain. When I heard the good report, this Baptist preacher responded like a Pentecostal!

For the next two years I had PET scans to see if all was clear. I know that "the just shall live by faith," and I tried to do so. But I also know that with this disease you live from scan to scan. When Dr. Legha released me, Veta said, "You two get over there for a picture." Dr. Legha responded, "Veta, send me a copy. I'd like to put it on my bulletin board. I don't have very many successes." We walked humbly and joyfully away.

The gift of a clean bill of health allowed me and Veta to savor the joys of watching our grandchildren develop and grow. By 2001, our family was blessed with six grandchildren. A funny thing happened at the supper table when Jonathan, Deb and Tim's oldest, entered the first grade. Out of the clear blue he said, "Mom, could I have an allowance?" They responded, "Jonathan, what is an allowance?" He replied, "Well, the kids at school say it is money that their parents give them every week. I don't have any money, so I would like an allowance." Debbie said, "Jonathan, what makes you think that we can afford to give you an allowance?" He said, "Mom, you do about fifteen operations a week. I think you must get at least ten dollars for each operation . . . so could I have an allowance?" Debbie and Tim tried their best to keep a straight face. Jonathan was unsuccessful in his endeavor, however, we all had a good laugh when we heard the story—just one of the joys of being grandparents.

Veta's father, Dad Cole, went to glory in 1998. He was a class act and an inspiration and blessing to us all. We worked on many

Donny and Jordan when she was seven.

Jonathan, age five

projects together through the years. I truly believe that I was blessed with two fathers. I officiated his service in the Woodmont Chapel, and he was laid to rest at Woodlawn Cemetery. I could not have asked for a finer father-in-love.

15
FIRST BAPTIST, FAIRVIEW, TENNESSEE

2001–2011

One afternoon in May 2001 the phone rang. A voice at the other end of the line said, "Dr. Sherman, this is Gene Elliott. I was sitting in your daughter's office and asked her how you were getting along with your cancer. She told me you were doing just fine and that you were preaching again. She said that we needed to ask you out to Fairview to preach for us. That's why I called. Our pastor moved to Estill Springs, and we need someone. Could you preach this Sunday for us?"

In 2001 there were about eight thousand folks in the city of Fairview, which was located twenty-five miles southwest of Nashville on Highway 100. The citizens were good, down-home folk, many of them tradesmen who worked primarily in Nashville and the surrounding towns. I knew their previous pastor, James Patton, who served them for fifteen years. Veta and I made our way to Fairview on the second Sunday in May where I preached the morning and evening services to 150 members. Virtually all of them had watched our worship services at Woodmont through the years. After the Sunday evening service Mrs. Lois Shelton handed me an envelope and said, "Will you come back next Sunday?" This pattern continued for about six Sundays. Finally, the chairman of the pulpit committee asked, "Will you be our interim pastor?" I said, "Yes." I continued in this capacity for the next seven months. An interesting conversion took place during those months. Charles Lampley, who was well-known in the community, began to attend church. In previous years he sat at home on Sundays tuning in to Woodmont's service on television. Charles had never made a public profession of faith. His wife, Dorothy, shared that she was so pleased he was coming to worship. One Sunday he came forward and accepted the Lord. Everyone was delighted. When I baptized him and brought him out of the water, half the congregation cheered while the other half was in tears. It was serendipity!

In December Harry Hughes, chairman of the pulpit committee, asked, "Would you and Veta come out Thursday night and talk with the committee?" We said, "Yes." On the drive out to the church Veta said, "Honey, what do you think the committee wants to talk about? Do you think they want us as the next pastor and wife?" Over the previous six months several church members had mentioned privately to us they would like for us to come. There were ten members on the committee. When everyone was there, we began with prayer. Then Harry turned to us and said, "Dr. Sherman, our committee would like for you and Mrs. Veta to be our pastor and wife." I was not totally surprised. I replied, "Harry, I think you all are crazy. I am sixty-nine years old and have cancer. I may be in the cemetery in six months." He grinned and said, "We'll take the risk." And that is how I came to serve as pastor of the First Baptist Church, Fairview for almost twenty years.

When I looked over the church, one problem stood out—the facilities. The meetinghouse, which had been built in 1982, was basically in good shape; however, the education space needed attention. The parking lot was unpaved and unlit. The church had over $60,000 available that we could use for a facelift. I challenged our people to do the work ourselves, and they came on strong. In a matter of months, working Monday, Tuesday, and Thursday nights, the membership got the work done. We painted every room in the church and recarpeted the meetinghouse. Another church gave us a dozen light poles, which we cleaned up, painted, and mounted. Behold—we had light. We had the parking lot paved. By the first of March the entire church grounds and facilities were complete. We laughed, talked, worked, and got the job done and, in the process, got to know each other. Incidentally, the crew bought me a new joke book when the dust settled. The change was good—for the facilities, for the members, and for the community.

In the first fifteen months that we were there, FBC Fairview gained 147 new members, and Sunday School attendance grew from 155 to 235. Now we needed a new education building. The church voted to proceed in 2002 at a total cost of $1,400,000. We broke ground in March 2003. Church members loaned the money and, in addition, volunteered and completed $225,000 of the work themselves. We dedicated the building in May 2004. Sunday School attendance was running well over three hundred at the time of completion.

John Bledsoe came as minister of music in 2004. Each of us was a part-time staff member. Lois Shelton was education as well as church secretary. Kim Sullivan was our financial secretary. Brad Coleman (2005) and Andrew Mangrum (2007) worked with the youth. On Sundays we had our regular services. Wednesday night was church supper, mission organizations, youth group, and three adult studies. Vacation Bible School was in the summer with more than three hundred boys, girls, and adults taking part. Members decorated the meetinghouse and every classroom to the extreme. In the fall we had special nights, with most every Sunday School class doing a skit that was some kind of funny. The church years seemed to go by so quickly.

A funny thing happened one morning during Sunday School. I was sitting in my office when the door opened; Brad Coleman, our youth director, came in laughing to beat the band. He said, "Preacher, you've got to hear what happened in the four-year-old department. They were singing a line of the praise song, 'Be exalted, He's exalted, be exalted, O Lord.' The teacher stopped and asked, 'Boys and girls, do you understand what we're singing?' Quick as a flash a little boy in bib overalls held up his hand and said, 'God's tired. He's just wore out.' Bless his heart. He had innocently been singing, 'He's exhausted' instead of 'He's exalted!'" I shared the story with the congregation later in worship, and we all had a good laugh.

Our church began an Upward football/cheerleading minis-try in 2007. The program was designed to touch people in the community who did not go to church. John Bledsoe was the mover and the shaker behind the scenes, though over eighty adults worked together to make the program fly. Upward became an annual highlight of the late summer and fall each year.

In 2008 we sponsored two work crews who went to the Gulf Coast to rebuild after hurricanes. In addition, a tornado swept through just south of Fairview that year, destroying houses and barns. Our church undertook the building of a house for a lady named Marie Mangrum. Her insurance provided the materials; our church provided the builders. The rebuilding took almost a year, and her house was dedicated in 2009. Everyone who worked on the house received a great blessing.

In 2009 we added a dinner theater to benefit our boys and girls who went to CentriKid, a Christian children's summer camp. Linda Wheeler was the director, and our members were the cast. The first year there was one dinner and performance. The fol-lowing year there were three dinners and performances due to the remarkable response and support from the community. The dinner theater is still going strong.

Also, in 2009 our church established a medical equipment closet for the community. Members donated walkers, crutches, and every kind of medical rehab equipment to the church to be loaned out to anyone in Fairview who had a need. People requesting the equipment could return it when they no longer required it, or they could keep it indefinitely. Folks needing sup-plies showed up by the score. We were glad to help them.

The year 2010 was a good one for the church. FBC cele-brated forty-five years of ministry. The former pastors were Larry Johnson, Alton Wilson, Milton Knox, and Jim Patton. Seeing the folks gather around and tell stories of yesteryear was a joy. When summer came our VBS set a record enrollment of 471 with an average attendance of 372. In 2010 we built our first Habitat for Humanity house. We never lacked for volunteers. Those mem-bers could make anything happen. In 2011 three of our members participated in overseas mission trips. These trips were just a start; others would follow.

One of the things I enjoyed about Fairview was that I could stand at the back door after worship and call each person's name. I knew which kids belonged to which parents. We were family. At Woodmont where we had 3,200 resident members, knowing each individual's name was difficult. One morning when I first started at FBC, Jonathan Bledsoe came out the door. He was about four years old. He knew I liked to tell jokes, so he had one for me. He said, "Dr. Sherman, do you know what you have if you have a cow without legs?" I said, "No." He smiled and said, "Ground beef!" I chuckled, and he walked on. About five minutes later his brother came by and said, "Dr. Sherman, did my brother tell you a joke?" I said, "Yes, about ground beef." He said, "Well, do you know what you have if you have a cow with only two front legs?" I said, "No." He said, "Lean beef!" Such were the joys of ministry at Fairview.

Within our immediate family from 2001 to 2011, there were joys, and there were sorrows. Donny's marriage dissolved in 2001. During the divorce proceedings, the judge gave full custody of Jordan to Donny, and they came to live with us. We had an entire second floor available, and Jordan grew up with us until she went to Baylor. Donny inherited his old bedroom, and Jordan had her own bedroom across the hall. The turn of events bruised us, but we enjoyed being all together.

A blessed event happened in 2003 when First Baptist Church, Joelton, Tennessee, ordained our youngest son, David, as a deacon. The service was meaningful, and we were certainly proud of him. Woodmont had ordained Donny several years earlier.

My right knee had troubled me for a few years, so in 2005 I scheduled surgery with Dr. Christie, one of the finest surgeons in the southeast. I went to the pre-op class where the instructor told us that in two to three percent of cases there is a possibility of a staph infection. I did not give his warning much thought. The surgery went well. I had been in rehab for about four weeks when I awoke one Saturday morning to big-time pain, unable put my full weight on my right leg. I had a staph infection. The surgery took place that day. Things went along tolerably well until the same thing happened again. A second surgery followed. Despite taking three kinds of antibiotics, the knee did not respond; and I had a third surgery. This time they took everything out of the knee joint and put in a non-load bearing spacer. I began a regimen of antibiotics that would likely kill an elephant. I had to walk with a walker for seven months, putting no weight on my right leg. I rode a three-wheeler around the church and preached from the contraption as well. Finally, the infection cleared up. Thirteen months after the first surgery, I had a fourth. Everything in the knee joint was now new. I began physical therapy for the third time; and lo and behold, the knee responded. I finally was able to resume my normal life in 2006. I can play doubles tennis, do yard work, and garden. And I now have a ton of empathy for those who have knee problems.

In 2008 Mom Cole, Veta's mom, died at ninety-eight years old. She was my mother-in-law for fifty-five years. Actually, she was my mother-in-love. I have heard people say they never had a cross word with their mother-in-law, and I can believe that because we never, ever had cross words. She was an incredible lady. She was also Baptist to the core and usually president of the WMU in any church where she was a member. She was also a fierce defender of her preacher son-in-law through the years. When we played the Texas Aggies in 1953 at Kyle Field, I fielded a punt. Their punter kicked the ball so high that the entire Aggie team was within five yards of me when I fielded it. I picked out #72 and ran over him. In the stands a guy with a Stetson hat sat behind Veta, Dad, and Mom Cole. He said, "Who is #40? If Coody had caught that punt instead, he would still be running." Mom Cole turned around and said, "I'll have you know, #40 is my son-in-law, and he made a very nice play. Thank you!" Veta said the guy almost swallowed his cigar and said, "Yes, ma'am. Yes ma'am," and shut up. I led Mom's service in the Woodmont Chapel and laid her sweet body away at Woodlawn Cemetery beside her beloved husband, Luther. We were so grateful we had her with us for so long. I surely did love that lady. She was a blessing.

In addition to Mom Cole's death, Dot, Cecil's wife, died in 2008 as well. She had experienced dementia for several years. At the time of her death, Cecil was in Houston where doctors were treating him for leukemia, and he was not able to be with her for her parting moment. I was there with Cecil. Genie, their daughter, flew back to Richmond and was at her mother's side when she passed. She called her dad and said, "Daddy, Momma's home." It was a hard moment. When Cecil was able, we all gathered in Richmond for her service. She was a true Southern belle and a Christian lady par excellence. I continued to talk each night by phone to Cecil. They were both so special.

Two years later Cecil, my beloved brother, died from a heart attack on April 17, 2010. Veta and I talked with him by phone on Wednesday night, and he was upbeat. He had not had any chemo for his leukemia for about a week. On Thursday around noon Genie called and said, "Uncle Bill, Daddy has had a massive heart attack and is in the hospital in intensive care." We rushed to Richmond on Friday. Cecil was on a ventilator and unresponsive. He died the next morning. His death was quite a blow.

Preacher brothers Cecil and Bill in 1997.

Cecil was an excellent preacher, teacher, and Baptist states-
man; and he wrote some of the finest Sunday School lessons ever
written. In 1965 he challenged First Baptist Church, Asheville,
North Carolina, to integrate, and after a year of discussion, they
did. He had the courage to warn the Southern Baptist Convention of the dangers of fundamentalism. The convention paid a
heavy price for not listening to him. He led the charge to create a
new group of Baptists, the Cooperative Baptist Fellowship, who
honor true biblical Baptist principles. Cecil saw the need for a
new Baptist seminary and urged Dr. Herbert Reynolds, president
of Baylor University, to create the George W. Truett Theological
Seminary at Baylor in 1994. Cecil embodied what it meant to be
a true Baptist and a servant-leader. He was a blessing to my life.
We held services for him at both River Road Baptist Church in
Richmond and First Baptist Church in Asheville. Those were two
of the hardest memorial services that I have ever led. He left an
incredible legacy.

Veta and I took a beautiful cruise throughout the Mediterranean world in 2010. Our daughter, her husband, and our two
grandsons joined us. Our first stop was Malta where Paul was
shipwrecked on his fourth missionary journey. We then sailed to
Crete and visited sites from the Minoan civilization before head-
ing on to Cyprus. In Alexandria, Egypt, we took a bus to Cairo
where we visited the Great Pyramids and the Egyptian Museum
with the embalmed pharaohs that likely spoke to Moses. In Israel
we docked in what had been a major Philistine city. We traveled
to Jerusalem by bus and visited many of the sites of David, Isa-
iah, and Christ such as Mount Olivet, the Garden of Gethsemane,
and Golgotha. Going north we enjoyed the Sea of Galilee. We
sailed to Turkey where we visited Ephesus, and then it was on to
Istanbul and the magnificent Church of Hagia Sophia built by
Emperor Justinian in the sixth century. The trip was an inspiring
three weeks that we would never forget.

Veta and Bill in Ephesus in 2010.

A victory for us Baylor Bears in 2011 was Robert Griffin III's winning the Heisman Trophy. He was the best quarterback in the land. Baylor had a great year, and the Alamo Bowl Committee invited them to their bowl in San Antonio. That Christmas the entire family was in our living room where we had "Santa Claus." My family handed me a notebook. That was unusual. When the time came for me to open a present, I opened the notebook. The first page had a picture of the Alamo. I thought, "This is strange." The next page had two plane tickets to San Antonio. Then it dawned on me what was up. The kids were giving Veta and me airfare, lodging, and two bowl tickets to see Baylor play Washington in the Alamo Bowl. Veta and I went and had a wonderful time. Baylor outscored Washington 67–56 with the Heisman Trophy winner, RGIII, as the star quarterback. The game was a good way to end the year.

The whole greater family on Veta's 80th birthday in 2011.

16
FIRST BAPTIST, FAIRVIEW, TENNESSEE, AND REFLECTIONS

2012–2020

I was beginning my eleventh year as pastor of First Baptist Church, Fairview in 2012 at the age of 80. Most of my preacher friends thought I might have a loose screw. They wondered why I was still at my job. I always agreed with the proverbial quote, "If you find a job you love, you will never work a day in your life." I cannot say that every day is a delight in the ministry; however, the good experiences far outweigh the bad.

We began a new ministry at Fairview in 2012 when two of our fine ladies began taking CDs of our morning worship service to those who were unable to attend. The recipients were truly grateful. Our folk jumped in and built a first-class portico to allow members a dry and attractive entrance into the church. Rain or snow, our people could enter dry and happy. We paid off all our debt in 2013 because everybody jumped in and made it happen. Being debt-free was a good way to finish the year.

FBC became a drop-off location for Operation Christmas Child in 2014. Each year our folk filled around three hundred boxes for this worthy cause. A refreshing experience happened for me as a pastor that year when a high school girl named Hanna came to see me. She was a friend of Jessica, who was in our youth group. Hanna said, "Dr. Sherman, Jessica has become one of my best friends. I see in her life something that I would like to have in my life. Would you tell me how to become a Christian?" I shared the faith with her, and she accepted the Lord and was baptized. After that Hanna became involved in our youth group. I have thought about what she said a number of times. If we live Him, others will love Him. I was so proud of both these young ladies.

In 2015 FBC celebrated fifty years of ministry with a day of celebration. Former pastors and staff folks came such as Alton Wilson, Milton Knox, and Charles Adlay. Afterward we had dinner on the grounds. The celebration was a delightful experience, and seeing old friends was wonderful.

Our church gave a record amount of $15,000 to world missions in 2016. We also purchased a house on five acres for future growth and development across Overby Road that we paid for with cash. In 2017 150 of our members pitched in and did a massive renovation of our meetinghouse. They enlarged the space, painted the building, and laid new carpet. Members bought twenty-two pews that they gave in honor of both the living and the deceased to replace the worn-out chairs. We upgraded the sound system and bought new choir chairs. The renovation was quite an undertaking, but the new facilities provided a marvelous environment for Christian worship.

In 2019 Roland Peavey led in the building of a prayer garden in memory of his lovely wife, Jeannette Peavey, who passed away from a malignancy. The following year Roland provided us with beautiful, stained glass windows for the meetinghouse. He enlisted others who wished to give windows as well. One could give a window in memory of a loved one or in honor of an individual. For instance, the Sunday School class that Dean and Lois Shelton taught for years gave a window in honor of their faithful service. The church was so grateful. That is the kind of good people that I served for almost twenty years at Fairview.

Another humorous experience happened in morning worship when I used a phrase from the pulpit that I learned from my farmer-grandfather. The phrase was "grinned like a mule eating briars." (Breyers is a brand of ice cream sold in Middle Tennessee.) An eight-year-old girl turned to her mother and whispered, "I didn't know that mules like ice cream." Her mother shared what her daughter said after church, and we both had a good laugh.

A strange phenomenon came to Fairview in 2020 called COVID-19. It had been spreading around the world for several months, hitting Europe especially hard. The World Health Organization called this disease a pandemic, a strange word to our

First Baptist, Fairview, in 2001.

First Baptist, Fairview, in 2020.

ears. Health authorities warned us that it was extremely dangerous. Within weeks COVID had spread to the point that we had to cancel church services. Many churches began to stream their services to their members. The medical community asked everyone to wear a mask and to keep their distance from other people. We had meetings at FBC to discuss what to do. Most folks agreed to follow what the doctors recommended. As pastor I could no longer visit hospitals or senior care facilities. I began calling our members on the phone. I went through the church directory twice, trying to stay in touch. The sick folk multiplied exponentially. Our daughter gave us insights into the disease. As

Veta and I were in our late eighties, we felt it wise to step aside not only for our sakes but also for the sake of the church. I tendered my resignation effective October 1.

The church gave us a gracious farewell with a worship service and dinner under a tent followed by kind testimonials. They gave us a generous monetary gift as well. Parting was difficult. We had plowed ourselves into this church family for almost twenty years, doing everything from preaching to sweeping to painting to trimming the hedges. The work was worth it all. We left the church not only free of debt but with a healthy bank balance. We truly enjoyed our time at Fairview and the wonderful people there. In retrospect the years seemed to go by in a hurry.

What events occurred within the greater family during these past ten years? Well, the Baylor women's basketball team won the national championship in 2012 and 2019. That was exciting! Baylor's football team won the Holiday Bowl in 2012. In 2013 and 2014 Baylor won the Big XII championship in football. Veta and I were co-chairpersons of Baylor's Heritage Club (a club for alumni who attended Baylor fifty plus years ago). Jordan, Donny's daughter, graduated from nursing school, and Jonathan, Deb's son, was a current student at Baylor. Jackson, Deb's youngest son, was in high school. Elijah and Jessie, David's sons, were in high school as well, and his daughter, Rachael, was in middle school.

The Sherman family with Baylor President Linda Livingstone and First Gentleman Brad Livingstone.

Veta, Bill, and Jonathan celebrating a Baylor touchdown in 2019.

Debbie, Tim, and their sons, Jonathan and Jackson, in 2015.

David's grown family and grandchildren.

Unfortunately, Donny suffered a critical brain bleed in 2014. The radiation he received for his melanoma had singed the capillaries in his brain. Twenty-four years later, the blood vessels in his brain became brittle and opened up. He spent several weeks in the hospital. Since Veta and I could not give him the medical help he now needed, we had to place him in institutional care. He rallied a bit; but as the months went by, he had another stroke. He was rational with us, yet he needed around-the-clock care. Every day Veta went out to the Meadows Care Center around 8:00 a.m. to help him with breakfast. She stayed through lunch assisting him. I spent the rest of the day with him, assisted him with supper, and tucked him in for the night. On Sundays Deb and David covered for us. Donny wanted to give Jordan away at her wedding on October 10, 2015. We could see that he was getting weaker. But he made it to the wedding in a wheelchair and gave Jordan away. That weekend diminished his strength, and he died on October 19 about 1:30 p.m.

I had led hundreds of memorial services, and now it was our family's turn. The service was at Woodmont where some eight hundred people filled the ground floor. Two of Donny's Fellowship of Christian Athletes buddies—John Stroud from Ole Miss and Jim Suddath from Duke—led the service. They were superb in painting a picture of Donny's life. We laid him to rest in Woodlawn Cemetery in Nashville. Donny was a wonderful Christian witness and an incredible son. Each person that his life touched was better for it. Through tears, our entire family thanked God for sending him our way.

As we all know, life goes on after the loss of a family member. Ours did too. The three things that helped us to move on were our faith, our family, and our friends. Psalm 23 says that we "go through the valley of the shadow of death," but we do not camp out there. Recovery does not happen in a day but is a process which God leads us through. I did not try to preach for two weeks. When I returned to the pulpit, the Lord and our congregation made it possible for me to do so. Slowly things returned to normal, and life moved on.

As I wind down my life and ministry, I have asked myself who and what have been the major influences in the shaping of my life. Without question, the first and most powerful influence was my Christian home. My father grew up as a preacher's kid and was a deacon as an adult. My mother's father was also a deacon. Both my parents were Puritan in their morals. Consequently, I was in church every time the doors were open. We attended Sunday School, Training Union, morning and evening worship services, Wednesday night services, study courses, revivals, RAs, church camps,

Mobilization Night for Church Training, citywide youth revivals, you name it. Through the years my parents taught us a pattern of churchmanship. When I entered Baylor in fall 1950 as a freshman football player, I continued to get up each Sunday morning, take a shower, get dressed, and walk four blocks to Seventh & James Baptist Church for Sunday School and worship. The pattern my parents had ingrained in me as a child continued.

Another powerful influence was my home church, Poly Baptist Church. Dr. Baker James Cauthen was the first pastor I knew, baptizing me when I was six years old. The folks in that church cradled me, taught me, encouraged me, and shaped me for eighteen years. Yes, I know it was the Lord who was responsible, but God used those folks to make a difference.

The Lord used Baylor University in a big way as a catalyst in fulfilling my call to the ministry. Christian professors like Ralph Lynn, Bob Reid, and Henry Trantham inspired me to climb higher. The youth revivals of the 1940s and 1950s provided a spiritual boost, while the songs of the era—"Christ for Me," "Turn Your Eyes Upon Jesus," "I'd Rather Have Jesus," and "Everybody Ought to Know"—kept us emotionally inspired. Seeing the Lord turn young people's lives around was a validation of the gospel.

Southwestern Seminary also played a significant role in my life. God used several professors to inform and inspire me. T.B. Maston, John Newport, Robert Baker, and Jesse Northcutt made meaningful contributions to my life by challenging me to dig deeper and plow straighter.

There have been scores of people in the six churches we served in these sixty-six years who have been a blessing to our lives and our ministry. I use the word "we" intentionally because Veta has made as much of a contribution to each church as I have. Everywhere we have served, the folks have always referred to us together as "Bill and Veta." Church members have loved and appreciated Veta as much as me and sometimes even more so when I have stepped on some toes for not behaving. She has both talked the talk and walked the walk. There are many wonderful pastor's wives and husbands and many who are just as fine as Veta, but none in my estimation are finer. I have thanked God through the years for her. When each church called me as pastor, it got two for the price of one.

Through the years there have been twenty-seven young people commit to Christian ministry in the churches we have served. They have served as pastors, missionaries, chaplains, counselors, and in music and education. I would like to share their names: Harry Rowland, Ira Reasons, Allen Reasons, Jud Reasons, David Moench, Chad Keck, Don Sensing, Will Sensing, Kevin Roberts, Jody Roberts Slaughter, Josh Moody, Russell Richardson, Harold Phillips, R.L. Calhoun, Ed Smith, Mike Bennett, Janie Tyler Sellars, Angie Hughes, Daron Butler, Chris O'Rear, Richard Suggs, Lillian Mauldin, Kevin Saunders, Debby Frey Smith, Vicky Dunwoodie McCall, Jerry Byrd, and Susan

Farrar Morris. Veta and I are so proud of each one of them. Their work means much to the Kingdom.

Life has been great for these sixty-six years. Veta and I would not trade our ministry for the world and would welcome the chance to do it all over again. There is a chorus that we used to sing during our Baylor days that expresses our feelings about our ministry: "I've never been sorry I answered God's call. I've never been sorry I gave Him my all. My life with the Master grows sweeter each day. I've never been sorry one step of the way." God has been good through the years. And . . . the best is yet to come!

Veta and Bill at their 67th Baylor Homecoming in 2020.

EPILOGUE

Those Who Came Before

The Shermans

As you may have gathered from these chapters, family has always come first for me and Veta. Given my passion for history, I have always had a keen interest in those who came before in our family. I realize that these pages are likely not relevant to most readers, but looking back has helped me trace the origins of the Shermans and their journey. If that interests you, I invite you to go back in time with my family.

Peter Sherman is my great-great-great-grandfather on my father's side. He came to America from England sometime prior to the American Revolution and settled in New York. As a teenager he enlisted in the 1st New York Infantry of the Continental Army, serving six years as a private in the Revolutionary War. For his services the government awarded him six hundred acres in Onondaga County where the city of Syracuse now stands. He promptly sold three hundred acres for forty dollars, perhaps because he needed money more than land at the time. He could neither read nor write but left his mark in records that survive today. He died in 1848.

Peter Will-Comeback Sherman was one of his sons of whom little is known. Peter's son, Charles Wesley Sherman, was born in Tompkins County, New York, in 1823. He was a farmer and a Methodist. Sometime later Charles and his wife, Maria, moved west, settling in Decatur County, Indiana. At thirty-eight years old he enlisted in the Indiana Corps of the Union Army in 1861. At dawn on December 31, enemy troops shot him in the leg while he was fighting in the first hours of the Battle of Murfreesboro. He lay on the field all night before stretcher-bearers carried him to a field hospital where medics pulled a silk handkerchief through his wound and poured coal oil on his leg. Miraculously, he survived. A rebel family whose home he stayed in for the next month nursed him back to health.

The United States government mustered Charles Wesley Sherman out of the Union Army in Louisville, Kentucky, in 1862. He returned home to Indiana and became the jailer of the community. Later the government gave him the position of postmaster, as a wounded veteran, in the small town of Brighton, Missouri; and his family relocated there. When he died in 1903 his obituary read that "he had seen the light—he had become a Baptist." Adjacent to his grave are seven smaller graves of his children who died in infancy. Only four children survived to adulthood including George White Sherman—my grandfather.

George W. Sherman was born in 1867 in Indiana. He and his younger brother Frank became Baptist preachers. My father remembered his daddy sharing with him how the boys played around the covered wagons in the evenings when they moved to Brighton where George grew up. While attending Southwest Baptist College in Missouri, he spent a summer driving mules to Columbia, Tennessee. Columbia, then and now, enjoys the claim of "Mule Capital of the World." After spending weeks in the saddle, the group rested for a week or two in Columbia before riding back home to Missouri. On Sunday George went to the First Baptist Church where he met a tall, attractive young woman named Sally Brownlow. On the second Sunday George asked for her address. They corresponded over the next year; and he returned the following summer, staying a month with the Brownlows. Before he returned to Missouri, George announced his engagement to Sally.

The Brownlows

The Brownlows originally came from the Carolinas. In the 1830s three Brownlow brothers migrated to Middle Tennessee, where one settled in Pulaski, another in Mount Pleasant, and the third,

This is my father's mother's family—the John Polk Brownlow family. Mr. Brownlow is in the second row with the beard. My father is the third child on the front row with the bow tie. He is six years old. The picture was taken in 1907 in Columbia, Tennessee.

James, made his home in Columbia. One of James' sons was John Polk Brownlow, Sally Brownlow's father, who had a long and remarkable life that he described in a handwritten, forty-eight-page autobiography written in 1912. In the 1840s he and his father took a two-month trip where they rode horseback down the Natchez Trace, took a steamboat to New Orleans, rode a paddle wheeler to Galveston, rode horses from Nacogdoches to McKinney and across Arkansas, ferried the Mississippi to Memphis, rode horseback across West and Middle Tennessee to Nashville, and finally turned south to arrive back home in Columbia.

In 1861 John Polk enlisted in the Tennessee Confederate Militia. He rode with Nathan Forrest, was wounded twice, returned home to heal, fought in the Battles of Franklin and Nashville, and mustered out of the army in 1865. Later, he and two other Confederate veterans founded the Maury State Bank, which still operates in Middle Tennessee today under the name

First Farmers and Merchants Bank. John Polk eventually became a lay preacher, holding revivals throughout Middle Tennessee. At the time of his death in 1915, he served as secretary-treasurer of the Tennessee Baptist Convention.

When John Polk's daughter Sally Brownlow married George Sherman in the late 1880s, she left her family home of Tennessee and moved to Louisville, Kentucky, where George attended Southern Baptist Seminary. After George received his degree in 1892, his first pastorate was First Baptist Church, Santa Fe, Tennessee, ten miles west of Columbia. His father-in-law, John Polk Brownlow, recommended him for that position. He served here from 1892 to 1896.[1] George went on to serve at three churches in Tennessee—North Edgefield in Nashville, First Baptist in Hartsville (where my father was born in 1901), First Baptist in Jefferson City—as well as pastorates in Oklahoma and Texas. His last pastorate was at the Polytechnic Baptist Church in Fort Worth, Texas (1920–1921). At that time Polytechnic Heights (Poly) was a small community five miles southeast of Fort Worth. George died in 1921 of a heart attack at the age of fifty-four. He and Sally had four children. An infant died in Santa Fe in 1893. Hester, Jeannette, and John survived. John was my father.

The Brannons

The Brannons were from the South. From a family Bible we know that Bridger Brannon was my grandfather's great-grandmother and that she lived in the Edgefield District of South Carolina. Later, the families moved to Georgia and eastern Alabama.

---

[1]   In 1968, during my first year as pastor at Woodmont Baptist in Nashville, I was sitting in my office when an elderly man, Mr. Walker, came in and asked my secretary if I was available. He had been a child when my grandfather baptized him at First Baptist, Santa Fe. His father was the country doctor that took care of the folks all around Santa Fe in the 1880s and 1890s. He spent over an hour sharing pictures and newspaper articles from a box of memorabilia that he brought with him about the church and my grandparents. He was the gofer in 1893 when his father and my grandfather built the parsonage out of ash lumber next to the church. During the 1980s I held two revivals at First Baptist, Santa Fe and was able to walk through that house.

During the Civil War, my grandfather's uncle, Llewellyn Brannon, was killed outside of Richmond in 1862.

We have no record of any of the family owning slaves. They were likely too poor to afford them. However, they died for those who did. My mother's father, James Harrison Brannon, was born in 1882 just outside of Anniston, Alabama. How he met my grandmother is unknown.

The Cooks

My mother's mother was Effie Mae Cook, or "Bamaw," as we called her. She came from the Pine Grove community a few miles east of Heflin, Alabama. Her father was the sheriff of Cleburne County. He lived a spirited life full of scrapes and shoot-outs, seeking to maintain order in his farming community. He died relatively young and is buried in the Pine Grove cemetery. His wife's name was Molly.

My grandparents, James Harrison Brannon and Effie Mae Cook, were married in 1904 at the Pine Grove Baptist Church. I grew up calling my grandfather "Dad" and my father "Daddy." When I asked Dad about his wedding, he replied, "Well, Billikin, it was on the front porch of the Baptist church on a Sunday morning. Effie and I stood on the porch with all the people gathered around. When the preacher finished with our vows, they opened the doors; and we were ushered in as honored guests and seated on the front row for the worship service. Afterwards, all the folks went to their wagons and got their covered dishes and put them on a long table, and we enjoyed dinner on the grounds. Then I went to my wagon, got my grip, put it in her folks' wagon, and we went to her parents' house. That was it."

My grandparents farmed land on the Coosa River where about every third or fourth year a flash flood washed out the crops. Some cousins, who had previously gone to Texas, sent back glowing reports on the farming there. My grandparents (Dad Brannon and Bamaw) boarded a train bound for Texas in 1906. They traveled with my mother (then a babe in arms) and Dad Brannon's mother, Molly, and Dad Brannon's three brothers, Lee, Henry, and Llewellyn. After traveling for two days and one night, they arrived at Handley Station, three miles east of Fort Worth. They made connections with kinfolks and became sharecroppers. Life was hard, but they hung in there; and a few years later Dad Brannon, my mother's father, was able to buy a sixty-acre farm for $1.25 an acre. The farm was eight miles southeast of Fort Worth, located in the Tate Springs community. My mother grew up on that farm, as did her younger sister, Ruth, and her baby brother, John.

My mother, Annie Mae Brannon, went to Little School, which housed grades one through eight and was across the road from Tate Springs Baptist Church. Dad Brannon, who was on the school board, wanted his daughter to have a high school education. The closest high school was Polytechnic High School in the southeast part of Fort Worth, which was eight miles from Tate Springs. So, Dad Brannon and my mother rode into town in their newly acquired Model T Ford. They stopped at the Poly Baptist Church and asked the pastor, George Sherman, if he knew of any family in the church that would allow my mother to board with them while she attended high school. He recommended Mrs. Young. They called her on the phone, and she invited them into her home. Mrs. Young and her husband agreed that Mother could stay with them. Mother worked in a bakery after school to underwrite her board. On weekends she attended Poly Baptist Church where she met the pastor's son John Sherman. A friendship developed, which led to a courtship, and eventually a marriage in 1926. The young couple lived in the former parsonage which the church had graciously sold to the Sherman family for around $400 in 1921 upon the death of their pastor, George Sherman. We three kids grew up in this house. Cecil Edwin was born in 1927; Ruth Hester was born in 1930; and I, Billy Don, came along in March 1932. In those days everyone had a double name in Texas. Such is my personal heritage.

Reflections

1. With the exception of the Brownlows, all the folk in my background were everyday people who had to work hard for a living.

2. All those who came before me were in the Puritan tradition. They were believers in God, church, family, and morals.

3. Preachers, deacons, and Sunday School teachers are common in my background. Consequently, when God called my brother and me into the ministry, our family was accepting, encouraging, and supportive.

4. My older brother, Cecil, said it well, "Though we knew few of them, they marked us. Since they were the way they were, we are the way we are. It may not be that simple, yet they were a powerful influence. We stand in gratitude."[2]

I wish to express appreciation to my brother, Cecil, for much of the background information on the Shermans that is shared in this epilogue. While pastoring at First Baptist Church, Asheville, North Carolina (1965–1985), he visited sites in New York, Indiana, and Missouri, to verify information on our family. He had a keen interest in our heritage.

---

[2] Cecil Sherman, *By My Own Reckoning* (Macon, Ga.: Smyth & Helwys, 2008), 13.

APPENDIX

Observations for a Meaningful Ministry

Preachers that retire are hardwired to give advice about the ministry. Some feel they may be authorities on the subject. I do not write from that point of view. I simply wish to share what I have experienced, what may be helpful, and what best to avoid. Some of these ideas may seem like common sense; however, I have noticed through the years that common sense among some preachers is not so common. Other ideas I wish someone had told me way back when so I could have avoided a minefield. Let us visit the 360 degrees of any pastor's life and work.

Pastor as Shepherd

No one can be a good pastor unless he or she truly loves God and loves people. We should reflect our love for God in every area of ministry. While I was reading A.W. Tozer years ago, his thoughts impressed me. In every heart there is a throne and a cross. When self is on the throne, Christ is on the cross. Only when we place Christ upon the throne and take up the cross will we truly be a follower in the faith. This message speaks volumes. When we truly love God, we will have time for people and will care about people, and people, in turn, will respond. The old saying is true: people do not care how much you know until they know how much you care. And in reciprocal fashion, if a pastor is there for a member in his or her time of need, that member will be there for the pastor as well.

A pastor should treat all church members the same. Folks will pick up on a pastor who has an inner circle of members that serve on all the committees and make most of the decisions. Remember that each church member is equally important.

A pastor must also live the gospel that he or she preaches. Edgar Guest says it very well in his poem *Sermons We See*:

> I'd rather see a sermon than hear one any day;
> I'd rather one should walk with me than merely show the way.
> The eye's a better pupil and more willing than the ear,
> Fine counsel is confusing, but example's always clear;
> And the best of all the preachers are the men who live their
>   creeds,
> For to see good put in action is what everybody needs.
> I soon can learn to do it if you'll let me see it done;
> I can watch your hands in action, but your tongue too fast
>   may run.
> And the lecture you deliver may be very wise and true,
> But I'd rather get my lessons by observing what you do;
> Though an able speaker charms me with his eloquence, I say,
> I'd rather see a sermon than hear one any day.

Be approachable with your congregation. Call each member by name. This personal touch makes a huge difference. A pastor can be a genuine friend to his or her membership as well as be their pastor. Finally, one of the best ways to live a moral life in the ministry is to set boundaries and to live within those boundaries.

Pastoral Responsibilities

First, remember that the pastor is the servant of the church, not the ruler. Christ settled this issue in Caesarea Philippi when he said, "I will build **my** church . . ." (Matt 16:18 KJV). Truly it is His church, and we are working to build His Kingdom, not ours. God calls the pastor to serve. In a Baptist church the pastor needs to recognize that each member is the pastor's boss. And while having specified responsibilities as defined by the job description, a good pastor will go far beyond that and jump in to make things happen. When a pastor works, his or her members will work.

Furthermore, the members will appreciate the pastor more if he or she is willing to do whatever needs to be done.

The pastor also sets the spirit of the congregation. If the pastor is loving, the membership will be loving. If the pastor is cool or argumentative, the church spirit will likely be the same. The best analogy I know for a congregation of believers is to be a family. John 1:12 says, "But as many as received Him, to them He gave the right to become children of God, to those who believe in His name . . ." (NKJV). If a pastor loves the membership as a family, he or she will not have a problem visiting hospitals, conducting memorial services, or officiating weddings.

A pastor has a great opportunity to make a difference in people's lives through counseling. He or she should share from Scripture and from experience words that will be redemptive to the situation. With God's help one should seek to be a blessing. On occasion a pastor must refer his or her congregants to professionals who have additional expertise.

In all matters there must be boundaries that ministers do not cross. Unfortunately, some pastors step across these boundaries. Nothing redemptive happens when ministers ignore these boundaries.

I would like to share one more idea on premarital counseling. Couples whose marriages I have performed through the years have come back forty or fifty years later and said, "One idea you shared, Dr. Sherman, that has really saved us from grief was how we relate to our new in-laws. You said, 'When issues arise, have the blood-kin address them with his or her own parents—husband to his parents—wife to her parents. Allow the spouse to be free of friction with the in-laws. Everyone has had disagreements with his or her own mother and father. They get over it because they are blood-kin. This method is a safe way to go and keeps a husband or wife free from conflict with the in-laws.'" I can personally share that Veta and I never had a problem along this line. She dealt with her parents, and I dealt with mine. We grew so close to our in-laws over the years that we would introduce the other's parents as fathers- and mothers-in-love. Each set of parents was a true blessing to our marriage.

The memorial service is another vital part of a pastor's responsibilities. The service has a threefold purpose—to honor, to provide healing, and to provide hope. As some attendees may never darken the door of a church again, it also provides a great opportunity to share the gospel. The spirit of the minister must convey the comfort of the balm in Gilead to the family. The privilege and responsibility of the minister is to share one of the greatest promises of Christianity—life after death. What a ministry.

Pastor as Administrator

Most pastors begin their ministry at small churches where they are the only staff member; and, as a result, there are not any administration problems. However, these pastors will eventually move on to a larger church with one or more associate staff members. The most important idea for all staff to remember is there is always enough love to go around. Every ministry is important in a church, and each makes a significant contribution. There should not be any rivalry. Each area of ministry is there to support and complement every other area of ministry. This concept goes well when all staff members are mature; however, some ministers along the way may be insecure or may not be team players. When this situation occurs, the pastor must step in and right the ship. With God's help, the staff member will solve the problem and His work continue in the right direction.

Another problematic area of administration is how to deal with a staff member who has morally stepped over the line. This situation can not only be a headache but can also divide a congregation—that is a serious issue. Several suggestions can be helpful. First, a pastor must do the homework and get all the facts. Second, he or she should bring in appropriate lay leadership, such as the chairman of the personnel committee and the chairman of the deacons, and inform them of the situation. Once these others have verified the charges, this small group should have a private meeting with the wayward staff member. The chairman of the deacons should conduct the meeting and be in charge of laying out the evidence. The meeting should be held in the spirit of Christ yet affirm that the staff member's behavior forfeits his or her position with the church. The group could offer the staff member two options—to quietly move on or to have all the evidence laid out before the congregation. Hopefully, the staff member will quietly leave. Know that the staff member's closest friends may side with him or her. People believe what they want to believe. At this time, the lay leadership who were in the meeting can affirm what occurred and why they took the steps that they did. All too often, some in the membership will blame the pastor, which is unfortunate, as the pastor is the one to bring healing. We live in a broken world; we simply must trust God and move on.

Pastor as Leader

We have already touched on the pastor as a servant leader. Another area I would like to address is growth in new members. If visitors attend a worship service, be genuinely aggressive and call them to let them know how glad you are they came. My pattern was to keep a page in a notebook with names and telephone numbers. Each Saturday morning, I spent whatever time necessary to call folks. I told them that there are many fine Baptist churches in Nashville; I never bashed a neighbor church. I then told them about our various ministries and let them know that we would love to have them if they felt our church was where they could best worship and serve the Lord. If they had children, I would have our children's or youth minister call them. Frequently, I heard that our church was the only one that had contacted them, though they had visited several other churches.

Another area in which the pastor needs to be the point man is missions. Everybody supports missions, but a lot of folks need to be informed and inspired to get the lead out.

The same mindset is true of Bible study. A pastor needs to be the catalyst to inspire members about Bible study. Have a systematic study of the New Testament. On Wednesday nights have an overview from a New Testament book. A good pastor needs to be a good teacher as well as a good preacher. Be enthusiastic! Inspire your members to get excited about Bible study. They believe the Bible, and most are happy to learn more about it. To sum it up, a leader must be out front challenging, inspiring, and participating to make it work.

Pastor's Family

I once read a thought-provoking statement that no pastor is a success in the ministry if he or she fails within his or her own family. The finest way for a pastor to inspire church members to have a Christian family is to model one. This practice takes work, planning, and commitment. The bottom line is commitment. Parents must demonstrate and model love in the home where the children can see, feel, and respond to it. They must teach right and wrong. Church leaders will teach it at the church, and parents can reinforce it again at home. Parents must teach discipline in the home and then require it from all. Each family member must learn how to work because we live in a work-world.

Family time can become a juggling act depending upon the size of the congregation one serves. When we were going to be at the church, we let the church help with our children through the multiple ministries for the various age groups. At other times I could be more flexible, as a pastor has the freedom to shift his or her schedule around. Each of our kids played sports. I would take in their games in the afternoon and then go visit in the hospitals at night. Churchmanship and family activities are not rivals; each is attainable. The key is for the pastor to put a priority on being home as much as possible. Family time is essential and pays great dividends.

Dealing with Criticism

I grew up in a Christian home where we attended church regularly, and I knew all my pastors quite well—Baker James Cauthen, E.D. Dunlap, Floyd Chafin, and Woodson Armes. They never seemed to run into choppy waters while serving. So I sailed through Baylor University and Southwestern Baptist Theological Seminary thinking that if I always took the right course of action, all would go well. That phrase became my motto. When I got clobbered for preaching that we should love all races as Jesus loved them, I was taken aback! Pastors must be prepared to face criticism. First, he or she must make certain that the criticized action was scripturally based. Was the pastor preaching the truths of the Scripture? Be calm in the response, standing firm and true to biblical truths. Be gracious to everybody and move on.

Community Involvement

Being friends with pastors of other persuasions is a wise investment. If a moral issue comes up in the town that needs to be addressed, the pastors can quickly form an alliance and respond. In Nashville, on two separate occasions, we were able to defeat local options to bring in organized gambling. Another reason to do so is to embrace those in Christendom who are a part of the kingdom of God. We Baptists are not the only saints. We will share Heaven with all believers who have embraced Christ as Savior, God as Father, and the Holy Spirit as our Comforter-Strengthener.

Pastor as Preacher

Preaching is, without question, one of the most vital areas of ministry. First, let us talk about attitude. We should affirm the great truths of the gospel with integrity, dignity, and a gracious spirit. A church member shared with me about a sermon he heard at another church. He said, "Preacher, his delivery was good and so was his content. But he came across with an attitude so strong that I told my wife, 'If I ever had a problem, he would be the last pastor I would go to.'" I realized that when a pastor preaches, he either builds a bridge to people or he burns a bridge with people. We should preach with conviction but also preach with humility and heart.

Second, know the playbook—the Scriptures. If a pastor is a lifetime student of the Bible, he or she will never run out of sermonic themes to preach. The pastor must believe in the message because the congregation can tell when a preacher truly believes what he or she preaches. Furthermore, the pastor must remember that his congregation measures the validity of the sermon in due proportion to the integrity of his or her life. The pastor must also preach the whole gospel to the whole person. Some pastors are one-note Charlie's—they preach only one theme of the Christian life. Evangelism, discipleship, missions, personal Christian growth, biblical literacy, and Christian witnessing are all-important themes that a pastor needs to address.

Third, illustrations are like windows in a house. They give word pictures to the great biblical truths. Sermons should not just be a verse-by-verse Sunday school lesson. All verses in the Scripture are the Word of God, but not all verses in the Scripture are applicable to today's world. You've got to make the sermon relevant to the issues of the day. So, all sermons should have some teaching, yes, but the best sermons offer clear ideas or takeaways that the congregation can apply to their lives. And the best way to drive these messages home is through stories. A sermon without illustrations is like a car with square wheels—it makes for a bumpy ride and a bumpy sermon.

Fourth, preparation and practice are key. The congregation can tell the difference between a prepared preacher and one who has not practiced enough. As you gain more experience, this process will become easier, but it's important to always do your best. One of the things I've found that really brings people back is when you memorize something such as a poem, a quote, or Scripture and recite it from memory in the middle of your sermon. Some of my favorites to recite over the years have included "Invictus" by William Ernest Henley, "The Destruction of Sennacherib" by Lord Byron, and "Light Shining out of Darkness" by William Cowper. This is in no way essential for all sermons, but when you do it, people will think, "Hey he or she really puts time into their preparation," and they'll be more apt to really listen to your message.

Finally, pastors should not hesitate to take a stand from the pulpit on moral issues. Many of society's moral problems have flourished because the Christian pulpit has been silent. The adage that "the only thing necessary for evil to triumph is for good men to do nothing" is true. The pulpit must declare conversion as an absolute necessity for humanity to know God—salvation comes only through faith in Jesus Christ—but the pulpit also must be prophetic, challenging the personal and societal sins of the day.

Stewardship of the Body

Through the years I have known some mighty fine preachers who made significant contributions to the ministry. However, because they did not take care of themselves, their careers were cut short. Some were overweight, others smoked, others lacked exercise. I grieved when they left us. I believe we should pursue healthful patterns for the body, soul, and mind to be of long-standing usefulness to the Lord.

To whomever may read this chapter, I hope it will be helpful. Sixty-six years of ministry have been a joy and a delight. I truly hope the same for you.

Printed in the USA
CPSIA information can be obtained
at www.ICGtesting.com
LVHW041211150324
774517LV00035B/1407

9 781481 319645